A Knig

Ewart Oakeshott, the son of one historical novelist, and the nephew of another, became interested in arms and armour as a boy; he started collecting swords while still at school at Dulwich. He now has a collection of medieval weapons of superb quality, built up with the aid of an unerring flair for good material, and, he says, the most remarkable luck.

In *A Knight and his Castle* Mr Oakeshott discusses the importance of the castle in medieval warfare, and describes the design, building and defence of castles throughout the Middle Ages. There is also a vivid account of the upbringing and daily life in a castle of boys training to be knights, and of their schooling in the arts of warfare and in courtly behaviour.

Written in an informative, witty style, the book is illustrated throughout by the author.

A Knight and his Castle

R. Ewart Oakeshott F.S.A.

Beaver Books

First published in 1965 by
Lutterworth Press
Luke House, Farnham Road, Guildford, Surrey, England
This paperback edition published in 1976 by
The Hamlyn Publishing Group Limited
London · New York · Sydney · Toronto
Astronaut House, Feltham, Middlesex, England
Reprinted 1976

© Copyright R. Ewart Oakeshott 1965
ISBN 0 600 35335 4

Printed in England by
Cox & Wyman Limited
London, Reading and Fakenham
Set in Intertype Plantin

Line drawings by R. Ewart Oakeshott
Cover illustration by Richard Hook

Contents

Chapter One

Earl Richard of Warwick

In St Mary's church at Warwick is one of the most splendid effigies of a knight that you could ever wish to see. It is made of bronze, gilded; it really looks just like a man in golden armour, so lifelike is the face and so carefully accurate in detail the armour; every bit of this, on the back as well as the front, is most carefully made; not a strap or buckle, not a rivet is missing. There is a sword on the left side; on the right there used to be a dagger but this, being easily hidden, has long since been stolen, as have the pair of gauntlets which once lay beside the sword. The knight's head rests upon a great jousting helm crested with a swan, and at his feet is a bear.

It was made in 1454, and is a lifelike portrait of the man whose body lies in the tomb-chest underneath it. His name was Richard Beauchamp, Earl of Warwick, and five hundred years ago his home was in the castle which still stands, and is still lived in just as it was in his lifetime, a little way outside the town of Warwick. He was a real man, whose effigy is certainly the work of a great artist, and the finest example in the world of sculptured armour.

The effigy of Richard Beauchamp, Earl of Warwick, in
the Beauchamp Chapel in the
Church of St Mary, Warwick.
It is made of bronze, thickly
gilded, and shows a Milanese
armour of about 1450

But look at the face of the man himself: would you think that this was a warrior, a tremendous swordsman and jouster, one of the leading captains of his day? More likely, if he wasn't clad in full armour, you might imagine that he was a thinker, a man of law perhaps or a writer, or an artist. We know a lot about his deeds, though – real, splendid feats of arms worthy of a Sir Lancelot – and there is no doubt that he was a great fighting man.

Long after his death, and after his more famous son-in-law, Warwick the King-maker, had been slain at the battle of Barnet in 1471, an elderly historian called John Rous, who had served these two Earls all his life, inspired one of his assistants to write a record of the deeds of Earl Richard. He called his book *A Pageant of the Birth, Life and Death of Richard Beauchamp, Earl of Warwick*. He had intended it to be a book of pictures with a little text, like a caption, to each page. A Flemish painter was commissioned to do the pictures, but the work was never finished. Only the text, and the rough sketches for the paintings, were done. These sketches as we can see them today look just like pencil drawings, but of course they are not, because pencils as we know them were not in use at the end of the fifteenth century. They were done with an instrument called a plummet, a sort of stick of lead pointed at one end which made a mark exactly like a 'lead' pencil does – except that the lead of a pencil is made not of lead at all, but graphite. Many years after the unfinished *Pageant* was left, the seventeenth-century historian Dugdale re-wrote it, though he added little or nothing to it. He simply modernised the spelling; I have done the same here, and modernised Dugdale's spelling in some of the most interesting bits I have taken to tell of Earl Richard's life.

He was born, heir to one of the greatest titles in the realm, on

25th January, 1381. At his christening his godfathers were the
King – Richard II – and the Archbishop of Canterbury, so you
can see what an important baby he was. We hear little about him
until he was nineteen, when he was made a Knight of the Bath
by Henry IV in 1400. Then begins the long tale of his deeds of
arms. At the coronation of Henry IV's new queen, Joan of
Navarre, in 1401, Richard Beauchamp 'kept justes in the Queen's
part, against all comers; wherein he behaved himself most
nobly'. This means that at one of the tournaments held in cele-
bration, he challenged everyone who cared to joust with him as
the Queen's Champion, and did very well. The same way, in a
more warlike manner, 'he was retained to serve the King for one
year with 100 men at arms and 300 archers'. This was because
he was one of the chief barons of the realm, and had to maintain
a band of trained fighting men to serve the King when he needed
them. And two years later, in 1403, need them he did, for he had
to face the forces of the rebellious Earls of Northumberland and
Westmoreland, led by Northumberland's son Henry Percy, the
famous Hotspur. Earl Richard fought at the battle of Shrews-
bury with the King and the young Prince of Wales (afterwards
Henry V) and after the battle was made a Knight of the
Garter.

Five years later, in 1408, he got leave of the King to travel and
visit the Holy Land 'for performance of a vow he had made, and
pilgrimage he resolved to take. He fitted himself with all
necessaries for that journey, and passed the sea. In which voyage,
visiting his cousin the Duke of Bar, he was nobly received and
entertained by him for six days; who then accompanied him to
Paris, where being arrived, the King of France then wearing his
crown in reverence of that holy feast, made him to sit at his table'

(kings in the Middle Ages wore their crowns ceremonially during the feasts of Christmas, Easter and Pentecost). 'And at his departure, sent a herald to conduct him safely through that realm of France.

'Out of which, entering Lombardy, he was met by another herald from a knight called Sir Pandulf Malacet, with a challenge to perform certain feats of arms with him at Verona, upon a day assigned and in the presence of Sir Galeot of Mantua; whereunto he gave his assent. And as soon as he had performed his pilgrimage at Rome returned to Verona, where he and his opponent were first to joust, next, to fight with axes, afterwards with arming swords, and lastly with sharp daggers. At the day and place assigned for such exercises, came great resort of people, Sir Pandulf entering the lists with nine spears borne before him. The Act of Spears being ended, they fell to it with axes, in which encounter Sir Pandulf got a sore wound in the shoulder and had been utterly slain, had not Sir Galeot cried "Peace".

'From thence he travelled to Venice; where being nobly received by the Duke (the Doge) and others, he had many great presents given to him by reason of the honour he had gained at Verona.' Next he went on to Jerusalem, and back to Venice again; then he visited Russia, Lithuania, Poland, Prussia, Westphalia and parts of Germany, 'showing great valour in various tournaments'.

He was back in England again in 1412, so he had travelled all these distances and visited all these lands – and fought in them – in the space of only four years.

As soon as Earl Richard got back to England, he was 'by an Indenture of 2nd October, 1412 retained with Henry, Prince of Wales, to serve him in peace and war, both in this realm and on and beyond the seas, for 250 marks per annum, to be paid out of the Princes exchequer at Carmarthen at Easter and Michaelmas, in two even portions. And wherever he should be in that princes court to have four esquires and six yeomen with him, and diet there for them all. Provided, that the Prince, in service of war, should have the third part of what he got in battle, and the third part of the thirds his men-at-arms should gain; and in case he took any great commander, port, or castle, the Prince likewise to have them, giving him reasonable satisfaction.'

This tells us a good deal about one of the jobs a great land-owner in the fifteenth century had to do. Barons like Earl Richard were not just luxury-loving millionaires, forever hunting and feasting and going to tournaments. They had important parts to play in the conduct and government of the country in peacetime, and in the organisation of its forces in war. This particular job the Earl was given when he got home had more to do with military affairs than with the business of government. But what exactly does it mean, that he was 'retained' by an 'Indenture'? A medieval indenture was a legal document, like a warrant or a commission or a contract. Two copies were written on a single sheet of parchment, one copy on the top part of the sheet and the other on the bottom part. The two halves were then separated across the centre by cutting the sheet in an 'indented' or wavy line; one copy was then kept by each of the contracting parties. In this way there could never be any doubt about the two parts belonging together; nobody could forge a copy or make a false one, since it would be impossible to copy the wavy line of cutting accurately. The two halves had to join exactly when they were brought together.

To be 'retained' simply meant that one was given a job to do for somebody – just as a history teacher is appointed to a school to serve under a head teacher, and as the head teacher is himself appointed to serve the local education authority. Earl Richard was given a post under the Prince of Wales, and to fill it properly he was required to have four squires and six yeomen with him all the time. A yeoman was usually some sort of fighting man, not of knightly rank but with some other 'trade', like a rating in the Navy or an aircraftman in the R.A.F. He might have been an armourer, or a farrier (a man who looked after the horses) or a cook or anything else. We can be sure that each of these yeomen was a specialist, a tradesman in modern terms, in some particular and important way.

The Earl was paid 250 marks a year for this service. A mark was two-thirds of a pound sterling. A mark in 1412 would have been equivalent to what one would have to pay for a good medium-priced Japanese automatic camera today, so the total of his salary would have been about equal to that of a top executive in an oil company – good pay; but of course out of it he had to pay his squires and yeomen, 'and diet for them all' – in other words, he had to feed them as well. This salary wasn't paid to him every month, but twice a year, half at Easter and half at Michaelmas. A condition of this service was that in time of war the Earl had to hand over to the Prince one-third of the loot or ransom-money he himself got in battle; if his squires or yeomen took any spoil or prisoners, *they* handed two-thirds of their takings to the Earl their master, and one-third of the third they had left they had to pay over to the Prince. If the Earl or his men made a very important capture – enemy commander, port or castle – it was at once given to the Prince, who would pay a suitable compensation.

A Knight and his Castle

In 1413, the following year, Prince Henry became King Henry V, and at his coronation Earl Richard was made High Steward of England, a very important office indeed. In the same year he crossed the Channel to see if there was any possibility of making a firm and lasting peace with France, and to discuss the idea of a marriage between Henry V and the King of France's daughter Katherine. This embassy failed, and within a few months England and France were at war again.

On the outbreak of this war in 1415, Earl Richard was made Captain of Calais. This was one of the key military commands in wartime. He was thirty-four years old, and now we can see the difference in his following. When he had his previous job in 1412, with his four squires and his six yeomen, he was just a member of the Prince's household. Now he was himself a high-ranking general with his own retinue of thirty men-at-arms and thirty mounted archers; 200 foot soldiers and 200 archers of foot. This was for peacetime. In war this increased to 140 men-at-arms, and 150 mounted archers; 100 foot soldiers, 184 archers on foot and four scouts on horseback as well as forty crossbowmen, twenty carpenters, five masons and armourers, bowyers, fletchers, farriers and other officers, as well as pensioners, 'for which service he was to receive himself 6/8d. a day, for his knights 2/– a day apiece, for the rest of his horse 1/–; for every mounted archer and every foot soldier, 8d.; and for every archer on foot 6d. a day for their wages'. So he got about enough every day to buy, let's say, a good transistor radio; his knights each got enough to have a moderately-priced dinner at a smart restaurant every day; his troopers a sum which would buy five gallons of petrol; his mounted archers and foot soldiers enough to buy a couple of pounds of rump steak every day; and his foot archers enough to pay for two modest rounds of drinks every day – though in these days of inflation and the rapidly rising cost of everything it is almost impossible to equate fifteenth-century values with modern ones.

When he arrived at Calais to take up his appointment, finding that the French did not seem likely to attack the town at all, he set himself to devise a tournament, and although I have said a good deal about tournaments in another book, it will be worth while here to describe this one, for the arranging and organising of tournaments was one of the most notable functions of the Lord of a castle or the governor of a city.

'He caused three shields to be made, one for a Green Knight, one for a Chevalier Vert, and one for a knight he called the Chevalier Attendant; all three must run a course with sharp spears. Each made out a challenge, which was sent to the court of the King of France. Three French knights took up the challenges and agreed to meet at a day and place assigned, which was a land called the Park-hedge of Guines. The first, Sir Gerard Herbaumes, called himself the Chevalier Rouge; the second was Sir Hugh Launey, who called himself the Chevalier Blanc, and the third was Sir Collard Fines.

'On the appointed day, the Earl, impersonating the Green Knight, came into the field with his face covered, a plume of ostrich feathers in his helm, and his horse trapped with the Lord Toney's arms (one of his ancestors) viz. Argent a Manch Gules. When first encountering with the Chevalier Rouge, at the third course he unhorsed him and so returned with closed visor, unknown, to his pavilion whence he sent to the Red Knight a good courser.

The next day he came into the field as the Chevalier Vert,

with his visor close, a chaplet on his helm and a plume of ostrich feathers aloft, his horse trapped with the arms of Hanslap, viz. Argent, two bars Gules, where he met with the Chevalier Blanc, with whom he encountered, smote off his visor thrice and broke his besagews and other harness and returned victoriously to his pavilion with all his own habiliments safe, and as yet not known to any; from which he sent this Chevalier Blanc (Sir Hugh Launey) a good courser.

'But the morrow after, the last day of the joust, he came with his face open and his helmet as the day before, save that the chaplet was rich with pearls and precious stones, and his coat of arms of Guy and Beauchamp quarterly, having the arms of Toney and Hanslap on his trappers, and said that as he had performed the service the two days before, so with God's grace he would the third. Whereupon, encountering with Sir Collard Fines, at every stroke he bore him backward on his horse, insomuch that the Frenchman said that he seemed to be bound to his saddle; the Earl, to disprove this, jumped off his horse and on again. But all being ended he returned to his pavilion, sent to Sir Collard Fines a fair courser, feasted all the people, gave to those three knights great rewards and so rode back to Calais with great honour.'

The Earl served with distinction in Henry V's campaigns in France, though in the *Pageant* nothing is said about his being at Agincourt. In 1420 he went again into France to arrange a marriage between the King and the Princess Katherine, but this time he went with 1000 men-at-arms at his back, and as we know the marriage took place that same year.

Another source of interesting detail about some of his daily doings is in one of his Household Account books for the years

1431–32. It was in 1431 that little Henry VI, now ten years old, came to France to be crowned in Paris; in this account book of the Earl's we come across several references to this visit.

The first entry in the book is for the parchment and covers for making the book itself, and there are many others such as 'For 3 Loads of Rushes bought of Halshide for the chamber of the Lord and Lady, 23/–', but more interesting are those referring to visits, such as ... 'Saturday, 23rd June. The King came, with 2 Dukes, 6 knights, 18 squires, and 20 yeomen to drink, and went away.' 'Monday, 6th August. The lord went away with 11 squires, 13 yeomen, 12 grooms, 8 pages and 26 horses after breakfast. Also there came Madame Talbot with 1 damsel, 1 esquire, a Nun of Laen, William Norreys, Richard Beauchamp, Mr John Upton to dinner and supper and went away.' 'Monday, 19th November. Of the marriage of James Dryland and Alice Lightfoot. There came Madame Talbot with 2 damsels and 4 squires to dinner and supper and the night. Also came the Earl of Stafford, Lord de Audley, Sir William Peyto and 10 esquires and 13 yeomen, also James Dryland with 8 grooms, Madame Blont, Madame Peyto, Madame Godard with 8 damsels, 6 wives of burgesses of the city, Hampton's wife, Borrows wife with 2 damsels, 8 burgesses of the city, Master John Upton, 4 of the kings yeomen of the crown to dinner and went away.'

There are other entries in this book which are interesting because they tell us something about the way people travelled: 'And in expenses of the Lady Countess of Warwick going by water from Rouen to Paris beginning on Saturday, 1st December, going by water and staying for 7 days and so to Friday on which day at night she entered Paris – with Madame Talbot, 2 damsels, 3 esquires, 1 groom, Madame Godard with 1 damsel,

2 yeomen, 1 page, 4 officers of the King, 1 esquire of the Cardinal with 1 yeoman, 2 armourers, with 54 persons, guests for the same time.' 'And for one "Schonte" (a kind of barge) hired at Rouen carrying the Lord's gear and provisions, viz. wheat, oats and fish with firewood and other things to Paris against the King's coronation ... and to 15 bargees hired for the barge of the Lord Duke of Bedford carrying the Lady Countess of Warwick with Lady Talbot and the damsels of the Lady with other damsels and with divers officers of the King from Rouen to Paris against the King's coronation with 10/– paid for bridge tolls. ... and given by the hands of the Lord and Lady to the Master of the barge in reward for his labour going from Rouen to Paris – £8/5/– Tournois.'

'And for 4 new wheels bought and made for the Lord's chariot with ironwork and nails and with the mending of the body of the said chariot together with the oversight by John Ball, with 4 traces bought for the same work. And for the making of 1 chariot of the Lord overseen by John Ball.'

There are many more entries of a similar kind, which show that travelling by road in chariots, which were four-wheeled coaches of the kind which were still being used in the time of Charles I 200 years later, was nearly as usual as travelling by water.

When John, Duke of Bedford, Regent of France, died in 1435, Earl Richard became Lieutenant-General of the whole realm of France – meaning of course the English bit of it, now much reduced, and what he could win back. The *Pageant* goes on: 'Whereupon, with his Lady and son taking shipping for passage over, and discerning great danger by a hideous tempest, he caused himself, with both of them, to be bound to the main mast of the ship; to the intent that, if they perished and were after found yet by his coat of arms discovering who he was, they might be buried together.' But they got safely to France. Here Dugdale adds something of his own: 'The state and lustre of his equipage in this journey may in some sort be discerned by his painter's bill. . . .' A transcript of the bill follows, which shows how much work a painter retained by a great magnate had to do. Mostly it is the emblazoning of shields and banners, great pennons for the ships and pennants for the lances of his knights, all aglow with the vivid colours of his heraldry – the arms of Guy and Beauchamp and Hanslap, the repeated device of the War-wick Bear and Ragged Staff, and all the other arms and devices of his family and household.

Four years later, in 1439, he died, one of the most influential statesmen in the country, and a beloved military hero. He was fifty-eight – not elderly by modern standards, but a good age in the fifteenth century. He died in Rouen, so his body had to be brought to Warwick Castle for his funeral.

Richard Beauchamp's funeral must have been a very magnificent one, although his tomb was not ready; indeed, the chapel which was being built to contain it was unfinished when he died. Not till six or seven years after was it complete, when work on the tomb itself could be started. The tomb was designed by one of the chief masons of the time, John Essex, a 'marbler' (sculptor) of London. Much of the actual work on the tomb was done by John Brode, a marbler of Corfe in Dorset, who began work on it many years before it was finished in 1454. The fur-nishing of the chapel was undertaken by two more leading crafts-men, Prudde the royal glazier who did the windows, and Richard Bird, carpenter of London, who made the carved desks with

The head of Richard Beauchamp's effigy, a most beautifully sculptured portrait. The 'Pattern' for this figure was carved in wood by John Massingham; the head would probably have been done from a death-mask of the Earl's face, unless it had been carved during his lifetime

panelled backs, which are still there, and a screen for the organ.

All the figure-work, and there is much of it, was done by John Massingham, a worthy contemporary of Donatello and England's most eminent sculptor at this time. He carved the 'patterns' in wood for the small figures which stand in niches round the tomb's sides – 'weepers' they called them – and in 1450 he began to make the life-sized portrait figure of the Earl in his armour to go on top. When the patterns were finished, they went to London to Mr William Austen, Coppersmith of London, who made moulds from them, and cast the figures in bronze which was then gilded. Massingham was paid £66 – about £5000 in modern values – between 1447 and 1449 for work he had done in this chapel, and we have the account for Austen's casting of the effigy.

You might wonder, when I say that this effigy is a portrait of the Earl, how it could be done accurately fifteen years after he was dead; he couldn't sit for John Massingham while he sculpted his face. The reason is because during the fourteenth and fifteenth centuries, and possibly before that as well, it was customary, when a great personage died, to make a cast in wax or plaster of his face. This was so that an absolutely correct portrait head could be added to the figure which, dressed in robes of state, would lie on top of the coffin during a lying-in-state or a funeral. In the museum in the cloisters at Westminster Abbey there are several of these 'death-masks' of our medieval monarchs. The best are those of Edward III (died 1377), Anne of Bohemia, Richard II's queen (died 1393) and Henry VII (died 1507). If you compare these, the actual casts of the royal faces, with the faces of their effigies up in the Abbey, you can see how the sculptor probably used the death-mask as a model. So it must have been with Earl Richard. Massingham would have carved his wooden figure with a death-mask of the Earl's face in front of him as a model. Before him, too, was a model for the armour. But what he used wasn't an old armour of the Earl's. He died, you remember, in 1439; Massingham was carving his figure in 1450–54. During these eleven years, the style of plate-armour had changed somewhat. This armour which we can see in St

Mary's church is one which would have been absolutely up-to-date in 1450; there are several real armours still surviving which we know could not have been made before this date, and in many Italian paintings done between 1445 and 1455 we see exactly similar armours.

Men such as John Essex and John Brode, and Richard Bird of London, were those who worked on the great castles. Famous and eminent architects who designed the cathedrals and abbeys designed castles too – in consultation of course with military men who knew what they needed, like Richard Lion-Heart, who was himself a wonderful castle-designer, as well as a fighting man and a fine poet and writer of songs. But the castles, which were centres of culture and the homes of wealthy people, needed to be furnished; and so in every age of castle-building the very best craftsmen and the finest artists would be commissioned to make the panelling in the chapel and the great hall, and the Lord's Solar and bedchamber, to do the glass-work in the windows of hall and chapel, to make tapestries to cover the walls, or to paint those walls which were not to be panelled or hung with fabric. These castles were not forts; they were the homes of the rich and noble.

Chapter Two

Castles, Squires and Knights

When we stand under the walls of a medieval castle, we think of war. In imagination we hear the roar and hubbub of battle – the clash of steel, war-cries, the creak and clatter and thump of mangonels and the splintering impact of the stones they throw, the rhythmic, deadly thudding of battering-rams, the hiss of boiling oil poured from the battlements upon the warriors in the moat, the rattling hail of arrows. If we consider the inside of the castle, we tend to picture fierce barons, surrounded by a horde of soldiery, armed to the teeth, feasting and drinking deep in its hall while miserable prisoners starve in rat-infested dungeons below, rotting in damp and filth. Such a picture, highly coloured and based upon romantic ignorance, is all the more difficult to wipe away because there is a slight element of truth in it. There were sieges, and ferocious fights below the walls. There were barons, though they were on the whole less fierce and more civilised than some stories would suggest – there were unhappy prisoners, too. But let us try and see the castle as it really was. For every day of warfare the average English castle saw, there were thousands of days of peace. Many castles were never besieged at all. The significance of the medieval castle is in the fact that it was not just a fortress, it was the home of a family. From the castle all the business of the local government of a district was carried on, and to it came a constant stream of visitors – not only knightly folk, but artists and craftsmen, musicians, writers, men of Law. There would be the masons who were working on the great cathedrals and abbeys, for instance; and these men, though they were called masons, were what we today would call architects. Many of them were very distinguished personages whose skill and advice were sought by monarchs – men who designed great and glorious buildings like the Angel choir of Lincoln Cathedral, the spire of Salisbury, Exeter nave, the great castles of Conway and Beaumaris and Carnarvon. There would be sculptors, like John Massingham; Chaucer must have stayed at many castles, so must Jean Froissart. These are men of the very highest quality – Chaucer, the great poet and story-teller, the admired friend of Richard II and his court: Froissart, a popular historian most rarely gifted – really more like a first-class historical novelist – a friend of Edward III's queen, Philippa of Hainault, and a companion of the Black Prince and all the great knights about whom he wrote so vividly. These, and their lesser contemporaries, were the sort of men you might find in a castle. There would be the musicians too, composers, instrumentalists and singers – men such as Benjamin Britten, Yehudi Menuhin, and Geraint Evans are today – and there were always the popular entertainers, in groups or singly, famous in their day as are the pop groups and singers now. Then there would be the great sportsmen too – jousters, swordsmen, and men superlatively skilled in riding or 'Venery' – that is hawking and hunting and woodcraft generally, which are paralleled today by the show-jumping ring and the race-track. There would be the great Captains, William Marshal, Simón de Montfort, John Giffard, Henry of Grosmont, Earl of Derby, Thomas Dagworth, Robert Knollys – the list could be endless. Suppose we imagine a group of guests at dinner in the Great Hall at Warwick on a day in 1357. The Earl, Thomas Beauchamp, is at home; with him are several noblemen of France, captives he had taken when he commanded the right wing of the Black Prince's army at Poitiers the year before; there is Mr Henry Yevele, the great architect who is working on the plans for the new nave of Canterbury Cathedral; Sir Robert Knollys, a famous and popular captain of mercenaries, who is home on leave from France; a great lady, an Abbess who is on her way to visit the King's court at Windsor; a group of musicians who have been sent for to join the Prince's court at Bordeaux, a painter who is working on a series of murals in the Earl's apartments, and one of the Justices of the King's Bench with his retinue of clerks and officers. If you translate such a gathering into present-day terms, you would have a great figure such as the Duke of Gloucester as host; a group of business magnates from West Germany; a leading architect; the General Officer commanding the British forces in NATO; the warden of a women's college at Cambridge; a well-known pop group, a famous R.A., and a Judge.

A castle was the place where such people, travelling about on their affairs, would naturally stay, though of course they often put up at abbeys as well. There would be others too, no less interesting, who would have an even more direct and practical effect on the cultural life of the neighbourhood. These were merchants, and the travelling sales representatives of overseas

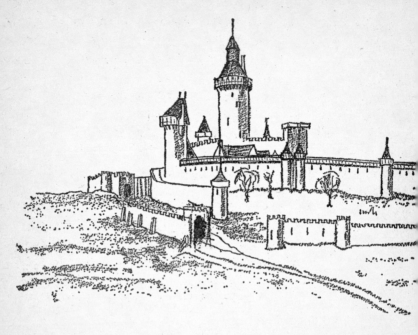

The Castle of Lusignan in France. This is drawn from a picture of the castle painted in about 1418; the castle was mostly built two hundred years earlier. This shows very well what a medieval castle looked like while it was still in use. The roofs are on all the towers; some are covered with red tiles, others with blue-grey slates or stone slabs. The great cylindrical tower in the middle of the castle, with its machicolated parapet and elaborate roof with many small gables and 'Tourelles', is later in date than the rest of the castle, and must have been quite new when the picture was painted. Adjoining it is the Great Hall and the domestic buildings

manufacturers. Let us not imagine that the Commercial Traveller is a modern character. His predecessors have been moving about all over Europe and Asia since the Bronze Age. Those who came to the medieval castles were the representatives of firms manufacturing or marketing luxury goods – Venetians selling

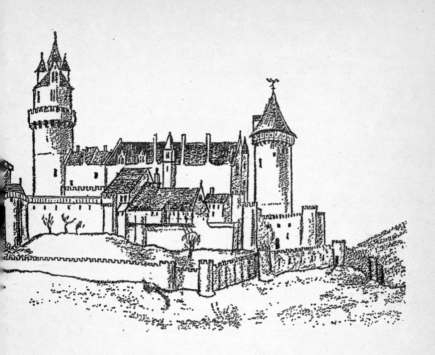

silk from China or ivory, or spices, or confectionery from India and Africa; rich velvets from Genoa and Florence, furs from Sweden or Russia, cloth from Flanders, beautiful leather goods from Cordova, wall-hangings from Arras, and armour and weapons from Milan and Augsburg, Innsbruck and Bordeaux – and, of course, wine merchants from France and Germany. To the castle folk, the armourers' representatives would probably have been the most interesting, particularly the Milaners, for from Milan came the best wares – so much so that the name given in the fourteenth and fifteenth centuries to the travellers has become the word 'milliner'. Armour was of course the Milaners' principal product, but they carried samples of all sorts of other things – clothes, hats and fancy goods of all kinds – as well.

Big armourers' firms like the Missaglia of Milan probably did a lot of trade in men's outfitting, and may very well have had great influence in the changes of fashion in dress, as we know that they were the arbiters of fashion in armour. So in modern terms the castle was a sort of mixture of private residence, strong point, Town Hall, art gallery and sports stadium – as well as being a magistrates' court and County gaol.

The whole of medieval society was controlled by the Lords, under the King, and the castles were the seats of their power. All this of course puts everything too simply. Many Lords had more than one castle, and many castles were not owned by the Lords but by the King, while simple knights did not actually own castles at all. The greater a Lord was, the more estates, towns, villages, castles and manors and forests he owned. His whole scattered collection of landed property was called the 'Honour'; the 'Honour of Warwick' for example, would mean the entire landed property, all over England and often with bits of France as well, of the Earls of Warwick. Where a Lord held many castles, each would be looked after and lived in by a man of high rank in his own following, who was called the 'Constable'. Thus many castles, and all the royal ones, had as well as their real owner a 'Lord' whose permanent home it was, and often this 'Lord', the Constable, was a simple knight. He would keep the peace in the neighbourhood, or make war in the interests of his overlord. Many castles were owned by the King; he didn't live in any of them permanently, but his lordship and control over them formed a great part of his power. In the many wars in England between the King and his barons, the success or failure of one side or the other depended a great deal on the control of the castles.

The Constable of a castle made it his permanent home unless he was moved to another one, or lost his job, but the great Lords who owned the castles moved continually from one to the other, visiting in turn each part of their 'honour'. So did the Kings, for they actually governed as well as ruled and all the time they rode ceaselessly about their realms visiting every part of them, seldom staying for more than a few days in any one place. They took with them an army of officers and servants, and an armed escort from the retinues of their household. There was always a group of the Lords of the realm with them too, each with his own following, as well as the great officers of state with their own households and their clerks.

The roads of Europe were full of movement, carrying this traffic of great households made up of men and women of all kinds and classes. The magnates travelled partly because they had to maintain personal control of their affairs, and partly because it was necessary to eat the supplies of estates as they stood. A great household, staying for five or six days on one manor or in one castle, would eat the place bare. If they stayed longer they would need to get supplies in from farther afield, with awkward consequences. Most rents and dues were paid in kind – so many cattle, or pigs, or so much wheat, so many fowls, eggs, fish, livestock and produce of all kinds according to the district. These things could not be preserved or easily transported; they had to be eaten on the spot. So when the taxes and dues of a district were eaten up, the household moved on. This constant travelling made the Lords familiar to their tenants and made the personal government of monarchs real and effective, for his constant presence all over his realm made a medieval king very close to his subjects.

The very first castles were used mostly as forts; the latest ones mostly as residences. During the seven hundred or so years of the Age of Castles, their use as homes grew steadily while their need for them as forts declined; even in the twelfth century we find their domestic side emphasised. Here is a description, written in the first half of that century by one Lambert of Ardres, describing the timber tower or keep which in 1117 was built upon the earth mound: 'Arnold, Lord of Ardres, built upon the motte of Ardres a wooden house, excelling all the houses of Flanders in that period both in material and in carpenters' work. The first storey was on the surface of the ground where were cellars, and granaries, and great boxes, tuns, casks and other domestic utensils. In the storey above were the dwellings and common living-rooms of the residents, in which were the larders, the rooms of the bakers and butlers, and the great chamber in which the Lord and his wife slept. Adjoining this was a private room, the dormitory of the waiting-maids and children. In the inner part of the great chamber was a certain private room, where at early dawn or in the evening or during sickness, or at times of blood-letting, or for warming the maids or weaned children, they used to have a fire. In the upper storey of the house were garret rooms in which on the one side the sons (when they wished it) and on the other side the daughters (because they were obliged) of the Lord of the house used to sleep. In this storey also the watchmen and the servants appointed to keep the house took their sleep at some time or the other. High up on the east side of the house, in a convenient place, was the chapel which was made like unto the temple of Solomon by its gilding and painting. There were stairs and passages from storey to storey, from the home into the kitchen, from room to room and again from the house into the Loggia, where they used to sit in conversation or in recreation, and again from the Loggia into the Oratory.'

At about the same time in England the historian Gerald de Barry (Gerald of Wales he is generally called) was writing a description of his own family's castle at Manorbier in Pembrokeshire, which reads very much like a modern description of a gentleman's country house in an Estate Agent's advertisement: 'The castle called Maenor Pyrr is distant about three miles from

Manorbier Castle, the home of the historian Gerald de Barry (Giraldus Cambrensis), as it is today

Penbrock. It is excellently well defended by turrets and bulwarks and is situated on the summit of a hill extending on the western side towards the seaport, having on the northern and southern sides a fine fish-pond under its walls, as conspicuous for its grand appearance as for the depth of its waters, and a beautiful orchard on the same side enclosed on one part by a vineyard and on the other by a wood, remarkable for the projection of its rocks and the height of its hazel trees. On the right hand of the promontory, between the castle and the church, near the site of a very large lake and mill, a rivulet of never-failing water flows through a valley, rendered sandy by the violence of the winds. Towards the west, the Severn sea, bending its course to Ireland, enters a hollow bay at some distance from the castle.'

These descriptions were written by men of letters describing castles which they had seen, but after the middle of the twelfth century written administrative records became common and many survive. From these we can learn how much care was given to the domestic parts of castles, and we see what the living quarters were like and get some idea of the life that went on within them. In the Public Record Office in Chancery Lane in London, there is a series of Rolls in which is set down, among other things, the expenditure on the royal castles during the reign of Henry II, Richard I, John, Henry III and Edward I, from 1154 to 1307. They go beyond this, but we are mainly concerned with these 153 years. These lists show how much was spent on living quarters in the castles, and exactly what improvements were made as time went on.

Medieval accounts were written on long sheets of parchment which had to be kept rolled up. The first set of these rolls, from 1184 to 1216, are called the 'Pipe Rolls' – because they look like pipes, rolled up as they are. The second kind, dating from 1216, are called the 'Liberate Rolls'. This name comes from the writs of 'liberate' set down upon them, that is, orders for the Exchequer to pay out (Latin *liberare*) certain sums of money, and the purpose for which they are to be paid.

The Pipe Rolls show, for instance, how Henry II built in stone a new royal lodging at Windsor, as well as a new stone wall with towers around the bailey. He built other residential buildings too, inside the walls of the great round shell-keep on the mound and in the lower bailey. We read of the King's Hall and his rooms, larders and kitchen; of the repairing of his and the

The Great Wall in the keep of Castle Hedingham in Essex. The arch spanning it from left to right in the picture is the upper part of the cross-wall which divided the keep into two sections. Solid in the lower floors, it was built as an arch in the upper floor to lighten the weight and give more space in the hall

Queen's seats in the chapel, of pictures sent from London to the castle, and of a garden made within it. At the same time he made improvements at Winchester – a hall with hedges set about it, work in the chapel and in the kitchens and upon a house for the King's falcons. Also there was painting done in the King's room, and a separate chapel to be prepared for the wife of his eldest

33

son. At Nottingham, a castle which Henry II gave to his youngest and favourite son John, a new hall was built between 1180 and 1183 as well as private rooms, and the keep was given a new timber floor. There was also a new Almonry (a sort of Estate office) and a mews for falcons, as well as gardens and a park. Henry II seems to have been fond of gardens, for he had one made outside his room at Arundel so that he could see it out of the window. King John seems to have gone in more for kitchens – at Marlborough and Ludgershall he made kitchens with ovens big enough to roast two or three oxen at a time in each.

During the long reign of John's son Henry III, a great deal was done to improve and enrich the living rooms in the royal castles. He was a great connoisseur and patron of art – his rebuilding of Westminster Abbey is the greatest monument to his taste – and one of our most fastidious monarchs in the matter of personal comfort and luxury. His favourite castle was Winchester, where he had much fine work done. He built the beautiful hall, which still survives much as he left it, and later had all the cracks filled in and the paintwork redecorated, his chair on the dais repainted and the paintings on the wall behind it renewed. In 1250 he ordered the Sheriff of Hampshire to have his new chapel painted and floored with tiles; to paint the table by his bed with 'images of the guardians of Solomon's bed'; to pave his room and the Queen's with tiles; to make wooden windows in the gallery of the Queen's chapel, and so on. He ordered tables and chairs and forms for his and the Queen's rooms, and had the Queen's room painted with green paint and supplied with new candlesticks and had a 'Majesty' painted, with gilded images about it, for her devotions. He also had a room built for his stewards, between the kitchen and the great hall. (The stewards were officials responsible for the proper cooking and serving of meals.) There was a new guard-room too, for his knights, a vaulted chamber which was to be wainscoted – that is, panelled all over in wood to keep out the coldness of the stone walls. This sort of wall-covering was still in general use up to the middle of the nineteenth century – is until now for that matter – and many panelled chambers survive in houses great and small. Several of these, dating from the seventeenth and eighteenth centuries, may be seen in the Victoria and Albert Museum in London; and apart from the actual design of the panelling must look very much like Henry III's new guard-room at Winchester. This practice of wainscoting the stone walls of castle living-rooms seems to have become prevalent during the second half of the thirteenth century, for over and over again in the Liberate Rolls of Henry III we find reference to it. In 1239, after the birth of his eldest son (later Edward I) he orders the Bailiff of Windsor to 'cause the chamber of our son Edward to be wainscoted, and iron bars to be made for the windows of the said chamber'. We need not imagine such rooms as being dark; most panelled walls we see now are of old wood which has darkened with age. We find that medieval wainscot was generally painted. At Marlborough the Queen's room was 'wainscoted and whitened', while one of the rooms at Windsor was to be 'painted of a green colour with gold stars'.

Glazed windows, too, were much in demand. At Marlborough, a new glazed window was put in the Queen's chapel, and in another of her rooms a window painted with a dove. At Windsor in 1236, when Henry married Eleanor of Provence, he had the Queen's Chambers redecorated for his bride; glass was put into two of the windows overlooking the garden, 'with shutters to open and shut', and another glass window in the gable was painted with the Tree of Jesse. Everywhere there was colour; today, when we look at the mellow stone of an Abbey or a Cathedral, we may not realise that when it was new it blazed with colour inside and out. Every piece of sculpture was brilliant in red and blue, green and yellow, while the gleam of gold-leaf shone from every surface. The west front of Wells Cathedral, built during Henry III's reign, with its numerous arches and columns and statues of Saints and Martyrs and Kings, is splendid now and beautiful because of the golden loveliness of the stone and the play of light and shadow over the sculpture and arcading. But what must it have looked like in 1250? Every bit of it was painted – the plain wall surfaces white and every column, every capital, every arch as well as every statue was coloured and gilded.

This passion for colour was by no means confined to the churches, for the castles received the same treatment. Why, do you think, is the great keep of the castle in London called 'The White Tower'? It is grimly grey now, the only touch of white being the stonework at the corners; but in the Middle Ages it was whitewashed all over, partly to look good and partly to preserve the stone. Most castles were probably treated in the same way.

Inside, as we have seen, the walls were panelled and painted; at Windsor Henry III had the cloister walls painted with pictures of the Apostles, under the eye of Mr William of Westminster, the King's Painter, and at Hertford Castle the walls of his 'Great chamber' were whitened and diapered in colours. A century later, just after the frightful calamity which men called 'The Black Death', when one-third of England's population was wiped out in a few months, we find that the splendid and extravagant Edward III ordered the Sheriffs of the southern counties to call up five hundred stone-masons and carpenters, glass-makers and jewellers to work in Windsor upon the Castle and St George's Chapel within it; and he had them fitted out with scarlet caps and liveries to prevent them escaping and taking other jobs. This outfitting was not wholly to make them conspicuous, so that if in a time of acute labour shortage they tried to get away to find better pay they could be spotted and brought back, but to give them gay clothes helped to keep them satisfied and happy in their work. They got good wages, too. In 1349 many English painters, in charge of Mr Hugh of St Albans, the King's Painter (a successor to Mr William of Westminster, Painter to Henry III) began to cover the walls of St Stephen's chapel in the Palace of Westminster with a frieze of angels with peacock's wings, and pictures of Tobias and Job and the Adoration of the Magi. These figures were shown in the Court dress of the time, on a background of gilded gesso. All round the walls were arcades with statues of silver-gilt, leading up to a great golden figure of the Virgin and a picture by Hugh of St Albans of the King and his sons being presented before the throne of God by St George.

As well as all this lavishness of decoration, fireplaces too had become a commonplace by the middle of the thirteenth century, not rarities as the chamber in twelfth-century Ardres where 'they used to have a fire'. In all the royal castles, Henry III was having fireplaces put into the living quarters. Even so, cold must have been an ever present problem. We read of the Lady Joan Berkeley, in Henry III's time, who 'in her elder years used to saw up billets and sticks in her chamber, for which purposes she

37

bought many fine handsaws'. Certainly one way of keeping warm, though the picture of elderly ladies sawing up firewood is an unexpected one.

In a household of this kind there would always be many boys of varying ages, being brought up among the fighting men and the ladies. A boy generally went into training like this when he was only seven or eight years old; at first he would be what was

One of the fireplaces in the twelfth-century circular keep at Conisbrough

called a Page, learning to be useful about the domestic parts of the castle, particularly with the ladies, but he would very soon begin to learn the duties he would later have to perform as a Squire, in the stables and kennels, in the mews among his master's hawks, and in the armoury. There was much to learn about the training and handling of horses and hounds and hawks; and in the armoury he would learn not only how to care for armour and weapons, but how they were made, maintained and repaired. This training would not be just theoretical, but practical as well. He would learn to ride, for instance – not just to be able to sit on a horse and get about on it, but to learn all the complete art of managing a trained war-horse in the joust and in battle. He would learn the ways of all the different animals that had to be hunted – hunted for essential food, not just for sport. And he would learn the management of different kinds of weapons, and how to sustain the weight of warrior's armour. Even at the age of eight he would begin to wear armour; every castle's armoury would contain many small harnesses for the boys in training, all of different sizes. (There are still a few of these small armours in existence, though most are later in date than the Middle Ages. There are however many swords of small size which have survived from as early as about 1250 – some suitable for a small boy of about seven, others a little bigger, for boys of ten or twelve. By the time a boy was thirteen or fourteen he would be quite strong enough to handle a full-sized weapon.) He would begin, then, to wear armour and wield weapons every day, getting his muscles accustomed to the weight, getting his whole mind and body used to the limitations it put upon his freedom of movement. Not that it was either very heavy or particularly cramping; it wasn't. You can move about in armour nearly as freely as you can in ordinary clothes, but by learning to wear it and use it from such an early age, by the time you were fourteen and became a squire, it would be as familiar to you as your own skin.

A page would learn a lot of other things too. He would be taught to dance, and to sing and play upon various instruments – how to compose his own songs, too. Some boys probably weren't much good at this, but many certainly were. He would learn how to carve every kind of bird and joint of meat; how to serve at table, how to handle wine properly and how to look after the comfort of guests.

When a page became a squire, his duties about the castle and his training would be much the same only harder, with more emphasis on the military side of it. While he was a page, if his lord went on a compaign and took him too, he would not take part in the fighting, but would help to look after the comfort of his master, and the knights who followed him, on the march or in billets; and in battle he would keep behind the fighting, with the baggage-train, and tending the spare horses, ready to bring up a remount if his master was unhorsed. But when he became a squire he would fight at his lord's side, and guard him in the battle.

The squire served the knight, and the page served the squire. At no other period except the Middle Ages has service for its own sake been regarded as ennobling. In ancient times, service was for slaves. In modern times it is only done, rather reluctantly, for high wages. But during the Middle Ages it was regarded as a high honour for a boy to be allowed to serve at table, or clean a guest's boots, or hold his stirrup while he mounted. As for carving the meat or pouring the wine, that was only for a senior squire or one of the household knights to do.

The actual training of pages and squires in these domestic and 'courteous' matters would be undertaken first, by the ladies of the castle, and by the chamberlain – a sort of glorified housekeeper – or in some special cases by the baron himself. But the essential fighting training seems often to have been in the hands of an experienced, war-hardened man-at-arms, not necessarily a knight but usually a 'sergeant'. This word was used to describe a professional cavalryman, who fought in the same sort of armour as a knight, but was not of knightly rank: a man who in modern terms would be a Trooper. Incidentally, you will find this word 'man-at-arms' (from the Latin *Hominus ad Armas*) very often in reading about medieval warfare. It was used to denote *all* men, knights and sergeants alike, who wore more-or-less complete armour and fought mounted – all Heavy Cavalrymen. Well, this sergeant would see to the boys' training in the use of all kinds of weapons – sword, short spear, axe, mace, dagger, pole-axe, pole-hammer and the cross-bow and the long bow – for a knight sometimes used these missile weapons as well as the archers. He had to know *how* to use them, for he might be in command of a company of cross-bowmen or archers. A commander who can't use his own men's weapons isn't much use. The long lance, as distinct from the footman's spear, is only for use on horseback, and the use of this weapon could only be learned on a horse. Of course they used sword and axe and mace on horseback as well as on foot; the other weapons, having long hafts needing both hands, were for foot-fighting. They would learn not only how to oppose sword with sword or axe with axe, but how to handle a sword against a man armed with a mace, or an axe against a man with a spear – opposing every kind of weapon with a different one. Experience of unarmed combat, too, could be essential, as well as knowledge of woodcraft and all kinds of country lore. The squire would also undergo all kinds of endurance tests hardening him to exposure and the rigours of the weather. When he was not doing any of these things, he would spend a few minutes every day swinging his sword or his axe to keep his muscles in trim. Somewhere in the castle bailey there would be one or two posts set up, about six feet (two metres) high, upon which the men-at-arms could practise their strokes, cutting at them with sword and axe. There were probably straw-filled sack dummies, too, for practising spear work on, like the Roman legionaries used to use, and like modern infantrymen use for bayonet practice. We know about the posts, because we hear about them in medieval tales and chronicles. There is a picture, too, in a fourteenth-century manuscript, showing a fully armed knight 'Practising at the Pell' as it was called.

Perhaps the most difficult of all the fighting arts was the management of the long lance on horseback. To be able to hit a small target, at a canter or a gallop, with a nine-foot (three-metre) spear tucked under your arm, is no easy matter. Not only do you have to aim your point at your target, you have to ride your horse at it too so that he brings you into the correct place and position for you to be able to hit it. Skill in horsemanship is not only combined with skill in using your weapon, but is an essential part of it. I have said something about lance-practice in another book, so I won't go into it again here.

In the chronicles of Jean Froissart, a contemporary of Chaucer, we find some interesting references to the part squires played in battle. For instance, in his account of the battle of Poitiers, fought on 19th September, 1356, there are several showing how a knight's squires fought beside him and looked after him after the battle was over, and how they came to wealth and position because of it. He tells us how Sir James Audley, one of the Black Prince's household knights, came up to him when the French began to advance upon the English position. He asked if he might have permission to fight in the forefront of the battle, instead of staying with the reserve near the Prince's person with his staff. 'Sir,' he said. 'Some time ago I made a vow that if I was ever engaged in a battle where the King your father or any of his sons were, I should be foremost in the attack, and the best fighter on his side, or die in the attempt. I beg therefore, most earnestly, that you will give me permission to leave your company with honour so that I can put myself in a position where I can accomplish my vow.' So Sir James set off and posted himself in the front of the line, with four squires who he had kept with him to guard his person.

Later, Froissart mentions Sir James again. 'The Lord James Audley, attended by his four squires, was always engaged in the heart of the battle. He was severely wounded, but as long as his strength and breath permitted he maintained the fight and continued to advance. At last, when he was quite exhausted, his four squires led him to a hedge so that he could cool himself and get his breath back. They disarmed him as gently as they could, so that they could look at his wounds, dress them, and sew up the most dangerous.'

When the battle was over, and the Prince was settled in his tent in Maupertuis village, he asked his knights if they had heard anything of Sir James Audley. They told him that he was wounded, and lying on a stretcher. The Prince asked if he was well enough to be brought to him; 'If not,' he said, 'I will go to him myself.' Two of the knights went to Sir James: and he got some men to lift him and carry him on his stretcher to the Prince's tent. They laid him down, and the Prince bent down and embraced him, saying, 'My lord, I have to honour you very much, for by your valour this day you have gained honour and glory above us all, and your prowess has proved you the bravest knight. And to increase your renown, and to provide for you so that you can continue your career of glory in war, I retain you from now on as my knight, with a yearly revenue of 500 marks, which I will secure to you from my estates in England.' 'Sir,' said Lord James, 'God make me deserving of the good fortune you bestow upon me.'

But he did a very fine thing with that 500 marks a year. When he'd been carried back to a tent which had been pitched for him, he asked four knights, who were near relations to him, to come to him. He told them of the Prince's gift, and then said: 'You see here these four squires, who have always served me most nobly, and especially so in today's battle. Whatever glory I may have gained has been because of them, and by their valour. I want to reward them; so in the same way as I have received the Prince's gift, I disinherit myself of it, and give it to them.'

*

Most people think of medieval knights in the same way as they think of 'cowboys', those heroes of the old days in Western America. These men are always presented in Westerns as young and fearless, handsome righters of wrongs and rescuers of distressed folk. We see them constantly shooting Indians and outlaws and riding about very splendidly, but they never appear to do any work, though of course we know quite well that real cowboys worked very hard. So it is with knights.

Let us see what they really wore, what they had to do, and how they got their living.

At first they weren't called *Knights* at all. They were just soldiers trained to fight on horseback in armour – mail and leather armour, not plate-armour. They were called simply, Horsemen. *Chevaliers* in France, *Caballeros* in Spain, *Cavalliere* in Italy, and *Equites* in Latin. In Germany they were called *Reiter* – Riders – which means the same thing. So why do we call them *Knights?* It is an Anglo-Saxon word, and to find out how these horsemen got this name in England we must go back to the times before the Norman Conquest in 1066, to the times when Europe was being attacked and raided on all sides by hosts of fierce fighting men. From the North came the Vikings; from

*A knight of the mid-fifteenth century, wearing a
full harness of plate*

the East, raiding into what is now Hungary and Austria, came savage tribes called *Magyars*, while up from the South the victorious Muslim Arabs drove through Spain and threatened France. The rulers of the peoples of Western Europe had to try and stop these raids and invasions from becoming an Occupation. The only way to do this was to raise forces of fighting men, well armed and trained to fight in the most effective possible way. And at this period the best way was on horseback, armed with lance and sword and protected by helmet, shield and mail shirt. It had been found that such warriors, acting together in troops, were able to beat Vikings and Magyars and *Saracens*. So every ruler had to set about getting as many of these *Chevaliers* as he could. He did this through his barons; he gave them land to hold in return for service to him. To perform this service, each baron had to build a castle and bring a certain number of fighting men to the royal army whenever he was called upon, so many Chevaliers and so many foot soldiers, according to the size of the land he held. Every baron had to be responsible for bringing in these soldiers. He *retained* them by giving them, in turn, pieces of his land which they paid for by service to him, and through him to the King. The piece of land held in this way was called a *Fee*, and the whole of this system of service in return for land was called *Feudal*.

It began on the Continent. In England, the Saxon Kings dealt with Viking raids and invasions in a different way. When a raiding force landed, everyone between the ages of sixteen and sixty was expected to turn out to fight; but they fought on foot, using the same arms and tactics as their enemies. There were no *Chevaliers*, so when Duke William of Normandy landed in 1066 with all his feudal warriors, the two different types of fighting force met; and as we know the old Saxon method was no match for the mounted *Chivalry* of the continental army.

After the conquest, King William had to reward his followers. He had no large sums of money, nor would his barons have wanted it if he had. It was land they were after, and land – English land, the property of dead or defeated Saxon lords – was what William gave them. On this land these barons built castles,

A Norman 'chevalier' of the late eleventh century. These are the men the Saxons called cnihtas

strongholds from which they held down the conquered English. The leaders of his army, and the lesser captains under them, were given lands to hold for the King. But they had to pay for it by promising to serve the king, each with his own following of fighting men. To the dispossessed and beaten English, these Chevaliers in the service of their Lords seemed to be just what they were – young soldiers in service. So they used the Anglo-Saxon word for such men – *Cnihtas* or Knights.

So in England a Knight was just a mounted soldier. And a tough, hard-bitten, hard-riding, hard-drinking, foul-mouthed fellow he was, of the toughest, roughest kind. What happened, then, to turn such a ruffian of the eleventh century into the gay, courteous gentleman of the fourteenth? Well, once the terrible raiding and savaging of the Vikings and Magyars and Saracens was held and beaten back, the people who lived in England and France, Germany and Spain and Italy – what we might call the whole of European Society – could settle down. They wanted a gentler and more civilised way of living. They were hindered though, by their own frightful warriors, the very fighting men they had produced to protect themselves. Now that they didn't need protection, the Chevaliers or Knights had no work to do. So of course they fought each other, and it was left to the Church to try and find an answer to the problem. One thing the Church tried to do was to decree what was called 'The Truce of God', which laid it down that nobody was to fight between Thursday night and Tuesday morning – a sort of long week-end off – on pain of excommunication. Naturally enough, this didn't work. Then, right at the end of the twelfth century, the Church was given a splendid opportunity. In 1171, the Saracens, not Arabs but a much fiercer people called Turks, beat the great army of the Emperor of Constantinople and overran all of Asia Minor, and Palestine and Syria as well. This was a very serious matter, and it will perhaps be worth while going into it in more detail. A large part of Eastern Europe (what is now Rumania, Bulgaria and Greece) as well as much of Asia (those parts round the Black Sea, with 'Asia Minor', now Turkey) and part of Northern

Syria, was still 'The Roman Empire'. In 364 the old Empire of Rome was divided into two parts, the Western Empire of Italy, Spain, Gaul and Britain, ruled from Rome, and the Eastern Empire ruled from Byzantium and Constantinople (now called Istanbul). When the old Roman Empire fell to pieces in the West, the Eastern half survived. It was this great, wealthy, populous Empire that, after 1171, was threatened by the Turkish Saracens.

Palestine, of course, mattered very much because Christ himself had lived and taught there. Christians from all over Europe went on long and difficult journeys – pilgrimages – to places like Nazareth and Jerusalem, and regarded the whole country as holy. We still call it the Holy Land. When it was overrun by these savage Turks, it was very serious. The Arabs, who had occupied it before 1171, didn't mind Christians and allowed them to come and go as they liked, visiting the Holy Places. But the Turks, Muslims like the Arabs, hated Christianity. They closed the Holy Places, massacred pilgrims, and forced Chrisians to become Muslims or die.

The Emperor at Constantinople appealed to the Pope in Rome for help. The Pope appealed to Christendom – that is, to all the people living in Christian Europe. He called on the fighting men to stop fighting each other, and to go eastwards to fight the Turks instead. This appeal, and the news of the terrible happenings in Asia, fired the imagination of everybody who heard it; so much so that from all parts of France and Germany masses of people, ordinary working folk as well as Knights and fighting men, set off on the long journey to the Holy Land.

Of course, they didn't all go. But this *Crusade* marked a turning point, for so many unemployed warriors went off that the

49

more responsible people who stayed at home were able to organise their affairs and the life of their communities on a better footing. And at about the same time, the land-holding classes in France invented for themselves another idea, which had a great deal of effect in turning the tough bully of a Cniht into Chaucer's 'verray parfit, gentil Knight'. They called it 'the Gay Science', what we know as 'Chivalry'. This set out a code of decent behaviour, among other things that every boy of a warrior family should take an oath when he was twelve, before a Bishop, that he 'would defend to the uttermost the oppressed, the widow and the orphan, and that women, particularly those of noble birth, should enjoy his especial care'. He also had to promise to defend the Church, and always to be ready to fight in its cause. As well as this, he was expected to be cheerful, always; to speak quietly and not to show off; to talk sense, and think, or not to talk at all; to be gracious and well-mannered – all those social graces that go to make a person nice to be with. All this he had to promise when he was twelve. He had of course to be a good fighter as well. Not just a good natural fighter, but a hard professional soldier trained to fight on his own or in company with other knights. He had to keep himself very fit, and be able to do things which today may seem to be beyond the strength of any man. He had to be brave, too. Part of his code was to fear nothing and nobody, ever. And he had to be loyal, particularly to his own Lord, his Monarch, and to the Christian Church.

So much for his code of knightly behaviour. What about his job? As in the time of William the Conqueror, he had to serve his Lord as a soldier. Not only in war, but in peace time for part of every year on garrison-duty in one of his Lord's castles, and for a time as a member of his Lord's escort in his constant journeyings. And of course he had to look after his own Fee, his land and tenants and servants. Among the people living on his land he often had to sit in his Manor Court and settle their quarrels and sit in judgement on their crimes. When he grew in age and experience he had to sit as a Magistrate in the Shire Court. He was a bit like a policeman, too, but really much more like a Deputy in the old West. He had to see that law and order was maintained, and if the Sheriff called out the *Posse Comitatus* he had to get into his armour and join his brother knights in his shire to hunt down criminals and outlaws. It was often a hard and dangerous duty. In England, though there were many civil wars, rebellions and national disturbances all through the Middle Ages, as well as a good deal of private warring between rival barons, a knight's duty was most often of a police kind.

Such, briefly, is what a knight was, and what he had to do. But suppose he had no land, no fee to hold, no 'Knight Service' owed to a Lord? There were many knights like this. The best thing they could do was to become simply professional soldiers and enter the service of some wealthier knight or baron as a retainer, getting their keep in return for their service. Whatever else they needed they had to win for themselves by their own ability. The main aim of any landless knight was, somehow, to get a fee or *Fief* for himself. Some achieved this by outstanding service, others by a fortunate love affair leading to marriage with an heiress. Independent souls would not bind themselves permanently to any Lord, but would wander about all over Europe seeking adventure and advancement wherever it was to be found. Knights who did this were called *Knights Errant*, or Wandering Knights. Actually it was possible to make a good living, even to gain great wealth and influence, by going about the world fighting in tournaments. To achieve this, all you needed was to be a good fighter, a gay and entertaining person, open-handed and generous, and a good companion. By the rules of war and of its image, the Tournament, if you were able to overcome another knight in fair fight and capture his person, you gained his horse and arms, and could get from him a ransom according to his means. If you were lucky enough to capture a great Lord you might make your fortune in an afternoon. Of course it was a risky business, for you were just as likely to lose all you possessed. Then, until you could find a friend or a patron to stand the expense of re-equipping you, you were in no position to fight at all. This was why you needed to be more than just a good fighter; if you could sing nicely, or play, and were the sort of person whose company others enjoyed, sooner or later you would find someone to help you. This was, more often than not, a lady. It was one of the graces of medieval society that the love of fair ladies was as good a thing, and as important to a knight's advancement, as military success.

Chapter Three

Castle Buildings

Man has always needed to defend himself and his property from the rapacity of his neighbours, and the art of fortification is very old. Everywhere you go, all over Europe and Asia, you can find traces of fortresses, some very ancient, some more recent, and many entirely modern. The castle may appear to be only one among these, but in fact it is quite different from any kind of fortification which came before or after it. The great hill-forts of the Iron Age Celts, the *duns* of Ireland and Scotland, and the Roman *camps* were fortifications in which whole tribes or armies could take shelter with all their goods and cattle in times of war. The *burhs* of Saxon England and of the Teutonic lands of Europe were for the same purpose. Ethelfleda, daughter of Alfred the Great, built the burh of Worcester 'to shelter all the folk'. Our modern word borough comes, of course, from this Anglo-Saxon word (Peterborough, Conisbrough, Edinburgh) just as 'chester' (in Manchester, Cirencester, Gloucester) comes from the Latin word *caster*. These were in no sense castles: a castle was the private fortress and dwelling place of a

Lord and his family. In European society during the late Middle Ages, from about A.D. 1000 to A.D. 1500, a period which might just as properly be called 'The Age of Castles' as 'The Age of Chivalry', these lords were the rulers of the land. 'Lord', of course, is the word used in England only. It comes from the Anglo-Saxon word *hlaford*. *Hlaf* was a loaf, and *hlaford* was a *loaf-giver* which suggests a kind, paternal protector, not an iron-fisted soldier. In France, the Lord was called *Seigneur*, in Spain *Señor*, in Italy *Signor*, all derived from the Latin *Senior*, meaning, literally, Elder. In Germany and the Teutonic lands it was *Herr* or *Heer* or *Her*.

The English language always produced words of its own, as we saw with the word *Knight*. This *loaf-giver* meaning of the word was in fact largely true in Anglo-Saxon times; and it must have been difficult and bitter to the conquered English to have to apply this name to the new, all-powerful Norman Seigneurs who ruled the country after 1066. It was these *Lords* who built the first great castles in England, and until the fourteenth century they and their knightly retainers spoke in Norman-French. Until the thirteenth century they thought of themselves as French, too; most of them held lands and castles in Normandy and Brittany, and their names were the names of French towns and villages – Baliol, from Bailleul; Sacheverell, from Saute de Chevreuil, for instance, and Beauchamp, Beaumont, Bures, Lacy, Clare and so on.

The castles we are now so familiar with are not much like the castles built by these Norman barons in their own country or in England, for these were generally constructed in timber, and not of stone. There are a very few early stone castles (the great Keep of the Tower of London is one still surviving almost unaltered), which were built at the end of the eleventh century, but the great age of castle-building in stone did not begin until about 1150.

The early castles relied for their defences mainly upon the age-old principle of the earthwork, and were similar to the ones that had been raised on the continent for the previous 200 years.

Reconstruction of an eleventh-century 'motte and bailey' castle. The bailey, here a separate enclosure, is surrounded by a stout palisade of timber, with a ditch all round the outside. The motte, or mound, has its own ditch, and a high palisade crowns the top, surrounding the timber tower. It is reached from the bailey by a long flying bridge, defended at its lower end by two small square towers. The upper section would have been in the form of a drawbridge. If an attacking force captured the bailey, the defenders would retire up the bridge into the stockade on top of the mound. The drawbridge would be pulled up after them, but the whole bridge would have been of very light construction and they would probably throw the whole thing down behind them

The first castles were built in the Frankish Kingdom as a defence against the violence of the Vikings. A castle of this kind consisted of an oblong or circular earthwork – a ditch and earth bank enclosing a comparatively small area – with a great mound of earth either at one end or in the middle. The bank was crowned with a stockade of timber, as was the top of the mound. Inside the stockade was a timber *keep*. Except for the mound, the whole structure was very like those timber block-houses built by the pioneers in the early days of the American West.

This type of castle is called the *Motte and Bailey* castle. The motte was the great mound which formed the central citadel – a word which later changed to *moat* and meant something quite different, the ditch encircling the whole castle. The bailey was the area enclosed by the outer bank and stockade. The timber keep built upon the motte was usually raised on four great corner posts, clear of the ground. There is a description of one of these castles in a biography of Bishop John of Terouenne, written in about 1130: 'Bishop John used to stay frequently at Merchem when he was going round his diocese. Near the churchyard was an exceedingly high fortification, which might be called a Castle, built according to the fashion of the country by the lord of the Manor many years before. For it is the custom of the nobles of that region who spend their time for the most part in private war, in order to defend themselves from the attacks of their enemies to make a hill of earth as high as they can and encircle it with a ditch as broad and deep as possible. They surround the upper edge of the hill with a very strong wall of hewn logs, placing small towers on its circuit, according to their means. Inside this wall they put their home or keep which overlooks the whole thing. The entrance to this fortress is only by a bridge which rises from the counterscarp of the ditch, supported by double or even triple columns until it reaches the upper edge of the hill.' The biographer goes on to say how one day, as the Bishop and his attendants were crossing this bridge, it collapsed and threw them thirty-five feet (eleven metres) into the ditch below.

The motte was generally from thirty to forty feet (nine to twelve metres) high, though there is an exceptional one in Norfolk, at Thetford, which is a hundred feet (thirty metres) high. It was flat on top and the upper palisade enclosed an area of about fifty or sixty yards (about fifty metres) square. The bailey varied in extent from about one and a half acres (three and a half hectares) to about three acres (seven and a half hectares) – rarely very large. The shape varied – some were oblong, some square, some shaped like a figure eight – there were endless possibilities of variation dictated by the wealth of the builder or the configuration of the ground. Once the site had been chosen, the first thing to do was to dig out the ditch around it; the earth dug out was thrown on to the inside of the ditch to form the bank or *Scarp*. The outer rim of the ditch was called the *Counterscarp*. If it was possible, the ditch was dug around a natural mound, but often this had to be raised by an immense amount of spadework.

Such were the castles built all over England after the Conquest in 1066 – we even have a nearly contemporary picture of one of them being built in the Bayeux Tapestry, where Duke William's men – or more probably rounded-up Saxon labourers – are shown building the motte of the castle at Hastings. The Anglo-Saxon Chronicle tells, under the year 1067, how the Normans 'wrought Castles widely throughout the Nation, and oppressed the poor people'. In the Domesday Book is the record of the houses which had to be demolished in order to build castles – 116 demolished at Lincoln for instance and 113 at Norwich. This sort of easily built fortress was exactly what the Normans needed to follow up their victory at Hastings and to hold down the hostile English, for they could go up very quickly. It is interesting to find that, a century later, when the Anglo-Normans under Henry II were trying to conquer the Irish, they

Dover Castle was built on a site where there was once a Roman lighthouse; the present castle was probably begun by Harold of England before William I finished it. In the late twelfth century great curtain walls with square flanking towers were added round the keep, with an outer ring of defences, most of which have now disappeared

built precisely the same kind of motte-and-bailey castles in Ireland, although in England and on the continent great castles of stone had by this time replaced the old earthwork-and-palisade ones.

A few of these new stone castles were new, on fresh sites, but most of them were rebuilds of the old ones. Sometimes the keep would be rebuilt in stone while the old stockade still defended the bailey, while in other cases a new wall of stone was built round the bailey, leaving the old timber keep on the motte. At York, for instance, the old timber tower stood upon the motte for nearly 200 years, long after a stone wall had been built around the bailey, until Henry III replaced it with the great keep, which still exists, between 1245 and 1272. A few of the new stone keeps were built upon the old mottes, though this was usually only

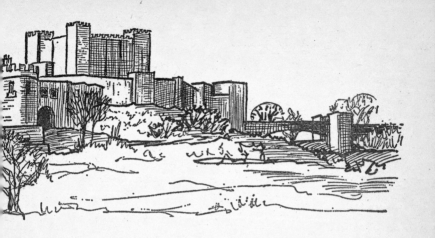

when the mound itself was a natural one; the great weight of a stone keep would be insecure if it were to have been placed on top of a mound of earth only dug about a century before. In some cases, where the artificial mound had not settled enough, the keep was actually built round it, incorporating the old mound in its own base, as at Kenilworth. In other cases, instead of a tower keep the old palisade on top of a motte would be replaced by a high stone wall enclosing the whole area of the mound's top. Inside this wall all the living quarters, storerooms etc. were built. Such buildings are today called *Shell Keeps* – the Round Tower at Windsor is an example, and good ones survive at Restormel, Tamworth, Cardiff, Arundel and Carisbrooke. The walls of the bailey were carried up the sides of the mound, as the old palisades had been, to join the walls of the shell on either side.

In England we are more familiar with the Tower Keep. In the Middle Ages this was more often called the *Donjon* or simply *The Tower*. The first word has changed its meaning, for no one today thinks of a castle keep when they speak of a dungeon; it has

59

come to mean the nastier kind of prison. And, of course, the reason why the castle in London is called 'The Tower' is because it has retained its original name.

The keep formed the central strong-point or citadel of the castle. On the ground floor would be storerooms for most of the food and arms in the castle; above it were the guard-rooms, kitchens and living quarters for the garrison, while on the upper floors lived the Lord of the castle and his family and retainers. The military role of the keep was purely defensive, for here within its unscaleable and immensely strong walls even a tiny garrison could hold out as long as supplies lasted. As we shall see, there were times when the keep of a castle was stormed, or so damaged that it became untenable, but these were rare; most keeps fell because of either treachery or starvation. The problem of water was seldom serious, for there was always a well inside a keep – you can still see the one in the Tower of London.

The shell-keep was quite common, perhaps because it was the easiest thing to add to an existing motte-and-bailey castle, but the feature which is absolutely typical of the medieval castle, particularly in England, is the great rectangular tower. The object of its design was that it should be impregnable. To this end it was of the most massive construction. The walls were tremendously thick, splayed out at the base to defy the picks, bores and rams of the besiegers, and rising sheer to the battlements seventy or eighty feet above. Flat buttresses called pilasters strengthened the sides and corners, at each angle rising to a turret over-topping the roof. The entrance was always well above ground level on the first floor, reached by an outside staircase set at right angles to the door and covered by a rectangular tower-like forebuilding set against the face of the wall. For

The Keep of Castle Hedingham, Essex, built in 1100. The steps leading to the doorway can be seen on the left of the picture; originally, a fore-building as at Rochester covered its entrance

obvious reasons the windows were very small. There were none on the ground floor, very small ones on the first floor and only slightly larger ones on the upper level. These features, the out-side staircase, forebuilding and windows, can be seen very well at Rochester and at Castle Hedingham in Essex.

The walls were built of rag-stone or rubble encased with outer and inner faces of ashlar or dressed stone, except in a few very early examples like the White Tower in London. At Dover, built by Henry II in 1170, the walls of the keep are from twenty-four feet to twenty-one feet (about seven to six and a half metres)

*The Keep of Rochester Castle, Kent. Built by
Henry II in 1165, it was besieged by King John
in 1214 and overrun when his miners brought
down the N.W. angle turret. The present
cylindrical turret was built to replace the fallen
one in 1200 by Henry III. The forebuilding can
be seen on the right of the picture*

thick; at Rochester they are twelve feet (three and a half metres)
thick at the base tapering to ten feet (three metres) at the top.
The upper and safer parts of the wall were generally a little less
thick, being reduced on the inside at each floor level, thereby
gaining a little in space and saving a little in weight and in stone.
In the larger Towers, such as London, Colchester, Rochester,
Hedingham and Dover, the inside was divided into two by a
stout cross-wall up the middle from top to bottom, the upper
parts of which were lightened by being pierced with arches. This

can still be seen clearly in the Tower of London. These cross-walls added strength to the structure and made it easier to floor and roof the building, as without the wall the spans would be too great. A cross-wall could have direct military advantages too. At Rochester in 1215, when King John besieged the castle, his miners succeeded in bringing down the north-west corner turret of the keep. The besieging force broke in, but the defenders got behind the cross-wall and held their half of the keep for some time longer.

The larger and taller tower keeps were divided into a basement and three upper floors, the smaller into a basement and two floors, though there are of course exceptions – Corfe, a very tall keep, had only two upper floors, so had Guildford, while Norham had four. Some, like Kenilworth, Castle Rising and Middleham, which were oblong in plan and not very tall, had only a basement and one main upper floor.

Each floor was devised as one large room, divided into two if there was a cross-wall. The basement was used for storage – provisions for the garrison and their horses and for its many servants, arms of all kinds, and all the stores necessary for the upkeep of a castle in peace and war – stone and timber for repairs, paint, tallow, hides, rope, bales of cloth and canvas and probably a good deal of quicklime and combustible oil, to pour over besiegers. Often the very top floor would have been divided by wooden partitions into small rooms, and in a few cases like Dover and Hedingham the main room – the hall on the second floor – occupied two whole storeys which gave a lofty hall with wall-galleries round it. (The keep at Norwich, now used as a museum, is arranged in this way and gives an idea of how it would have looked.) In the more important keeps there were fireplaces in the upper storeys and many good early examples survive. Where there was no fireplace, the chamber was probably heated by a large iron brazier.

The staircases giving access to the different floors were built specially in the angles of the keep, and were continued up into the turrets so that the roof could be reached. These staircases spiralled upwards in a clockwise direction; this was deliberate, for if any defenders had to fight on the stairs because an enemy had broken into the keep at ground level, they would have a double advantage; they would be trying to push their assailants down the stairs, and they would have their left sides, where they carried their shields, against the central pillar of the stair, while on their right would be plenty of space, even in a narrow stairway, to swing their weapons. The attackers would have to fight their way up, their weapons always hampered by the central pillar. Try this next time you are on a castle stair and you will see what I mean.

In the upper levels of a keep many small chambers were hollowed out in the thickness of the walls, private rooms where the Lord of the castle and his family and guests might sleep; and in the same way the latrines were built into the thickness of the walls. These were skilfully designed; medieval sanitation was very much better than we like to think. The lavatories in a medieval castle were very much more satisfactory and easier to keep clean than the old-fashioned earth-closets which can still be found in use in country places. They were small chambers built out to overhang the wall, open underneath. The necessary seats were built of wood over these openings, and everything went straight out into the air. They used to call the latrine the *Garderobe*, a polite word for it, meaning literally 'Guard your robe'.

In the same way the Elizabethans called their lavatories 'The Jakes' and we politely refer to 'The Loo'.

A well was of course an absolutely essential feature in a castle keep. Sometimes, as in the Tower of London, this came up in the basement, but in many keeps it was carried right up into the residential floors, which was safer and more convenient. Another thing which was considered essential was a chapel in case the garrison was cut off in the keep after the bailey, where the main chapel was, had fallen. The beautiful chapel in the White Tower in London is the finest surviving example of a chapel built within a keep; its more usual place was in the forebuilding, a small and simple chamber over the doorway.

Late in the twelfth century some important changes began to take place in the design of Tower keeps. The rectangular tower, massively strong though it was, had one weakness – its sharp angles. The stones in these corners could be picked and battered away, while the attackers who worked at them were almost invisible, and quite un-reachable, except from the turret immediately above. To do away with this risk and disadvantage to the defence, many keeps were built on a circular plan, and great cylindrical towers like the keep at Pembroke built in 1200 by William Marshal began to rise. Some were of a transitional kind, a sort of compromise between the old rectangular design and the new cylindrical one; these had many sides and no sharp angles. Examples are the keeps at Orford in Suffolk and Conisborough in Yorkshire, the former built by Henry II between 1165 and 1173, the latter by his half-brother Earl Hamelin de Warenne during the 1190s.

The stone walls which replaced the old stockades round the baileys were built on the same military principles as the keeps.

A reconstruction of a flanking tower and the walls of a thirteenth-century bailey. The tower is cylindrical on the outside, facing the field, but flat on the inner side. There is a small crane on the wall at the back of the tower for hoisting up ammunition to the defenders working in the hoarding. The high roof is built of stout timbers covered with tiles or stone shingles, or slates. The top of the tower below the roof has its timber hoardings in position. You can see how an attacker, having crossed the moat, would be exposed to the shot of archers in the tower as well as from the hoardings above. The rampart walk is shown, on the walls, as well as some of the lean-to buildings against the inside of the wall

They were as high and as thick as possible; the lower part was generally splayed out, to give strength to the most vulnerable part and to provide a sloping surface from which stones and other missiles dropped from above would splinter and ricochet out among the attackers at the foot of the wall. The top was crenellated – that is, finished with what we today call *Battlements*. This crenellation was devised like this: along the top of the wall was a fairly broad walk or platform, called in Latin *Alatorium* from which it derived its technical name of *allure*. On the outside this was protected by another wall, a parapet about seven to eight feet (two to two and a half metres) high, broken by openings at regular intervals. These openings are called *embrasures* and the pieces of parapet between them are called *merlons*. The openings allowed the defenders to shoot down upon their assailants, or drop things, but they had to expose themselves to do so before dodging back into the cover provided by the merlons. For this reason the merlons themselves were often provided with *arrow-slits* through which the defenders could shoot from cover. These arrow-slits were long, very narrow openings set vertically in the wall or merlon, only about two or three inches (five to seven centimetres) wide at the outside but opening out inside to give room for a bowman to use his weapon. They were about six feet (about two metres) deep, with a short cross-slit set a little above half-way up to allow the archers to shoot sideways at an angle of about forty-five degrees. There were many variations in the actual shape of these slits, but the principle was always the same. You can imagine how difficult it would have been for an attacking archer or crossbowman to shoot an arrow or a bolt through one of these slits, but if next time you visit a castle you stand on the inside of an arrow slit yourself you will see how well you can see the 'field' below your wall and how much room there is in the arrow-slit for you to handle your bow or crossbow.

Of course, a perfectly plain wall encircling the bailey would have many disadvantages, for once the attackers reached the foot of it you couldn't really get at them. If you leaned right out of the embrasures you would be shot; if you kept under the cover of the merlons you couldn't see the foot of the wall or shoot down to it. So it was better to break the wall at intervals with towers or 'bastions' which projected forward into the field, and from

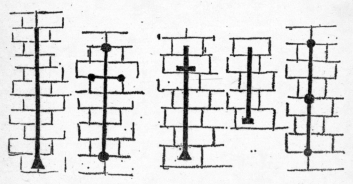

Various kinds of arrow-slits. In many castles there are different sorts of arrow-slits in different parts of the castle. Most had short transverse slits to allow a bowman to shoot a little sideways, but many were made without these. They were generally between four feet and seven feet (one and two metres) long

arrow-slits in their sides or from their battlements you could shoot sideways along the wall, thus 'enfilading' (as it is called) your enemy at the foot of it. These towers were at first rectangular, but later made in the form of half-cylinders set against the wall, the inside of each bastion flush with the flat inner face of the bailey wall. They were carried up to over-top the wall, thus breaking up the parapet walk into sections. The walk passed through each bastion, but these passages were closed by stout

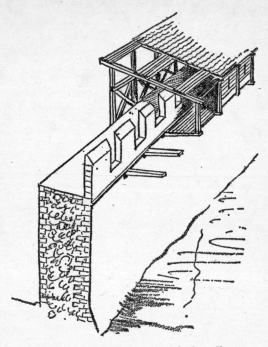

Diagram showing the way that the hoardings, or 'Brattices', were added to the bailey walls. These were probably only put up when the castle was likely to be besieged. In many castle walls you can still see the square holes, just below the battlements, where the great horizontal beams which held up the hoardings were put

doors. So if an assault party got up to the top of a part of the wall, it could be cut off between two towers and destroyed.

The castles we see in England today are usually unroofed and flat on top, except for the battlements, but when they were in use the towers and bastions were often capped by steep roofs, as one may so often see on the Continent. We tend to forget, when we look at a ruined castle like Usk, or Dover, or Conisborough, what a great deal of perishable woodwork and roofing there would have been. Often the tops – the parapet walks – of bailey walls, towers and even keeps were capped with long wooden galleries, roofed over, called *Hoardings* (Latin *Hurdicia*), or *Brattices*. These galleries were built out to project about six feet (about two metres) forward over the outer face of the wall; openings were made in the floor of this projecting part through which sundry things like quicklime, lumps of rock, boiling fat, boiling water and arrows could be sent down to the attacking force. The disadvantages of these timber hoardings was that they could easily be broken down by the stones hurled from the besiegers' 'Engines', and were easily burnt.

The most vulnerable part of a bailey wall was its gate, and right from the beginning this was given extra defences. The earliest of these were in the form of strong, square towers containing the gate; a good example is the eleventh-century gate at Exeter which still survives. During the thirteenth century most of these square gatehouses were converted into keeps by blocking up the gates and adding extra storeys, as at Richmond and Ludlow. In the twelfth century a more usual way of defending the gate was to build a large tower on either side of the gateway, and in the thirteenth the gatehouse proper appears. The twin flanking towers are now joined solidly together above the gate, and the whole thing becomes a strong and massive unit, and one of the most important features in the whole castle. The gateway itself has become quite a long and narrow entrance passage, blocked at either end by a portcullis. This is a gate which slides vertically up and down in grooves cut in the stonework at each side. It was made in the form of a great grid or grille of heavy timber, the bottom ends of the vertical members being cut into points and shod with iron – thus the bottom edge of the portcullis is a row of great iron spikes. The portcullis was moved by thick ropes working on a winch which was housed in the chamber above the entrance passage; in the 'Bloody Tower' in the Tower of London you can see the portcullis and its machinery. The entrance passage was further defended by *meurtrieres,* or 'murder-holes' pierced in the vault above through which the defenders could drop the usual things upon anyone who tried to force the gates – though it is likely that the primary purpose of these holes was to enable the defenders to pour down water to quench fires in the passage, for by far the best way to force an entry was to stuff the passage full of straw, brushwood and so on, preferably well soaked in fat, set fire to it and burn the portcullis and roast the defenders in the chambers above. Along each side of many entrance passages were narrow chambers built in the wall, with small horizontal arrow-slits giving on to the passage, through which a few crossbowmen could shoot at horribly close range into the packed mass of assailants in the passage as they tried to break in.

In the upper parts of these gatehouses were guard-rooms and often residential apartments, and in special chambers in the towers were the winches which worked the great chains for raising and lowering the drawbridge.

Because the gate was the place where an assault was most often made, it often had extra defences, called the *Barbican,* built out in front of it. This usually consisted of two long, high walls running parallel forward from the gate, thus forcing an attack to approach the gate through a narrow passage, exposed all the while to the shot of archers on the gatehouse and on the battlemented walls of the barbican. Sometimes, to make the approach even more hazardous, the passage was set at an angle to the gate, forcing the attackers to come from the right of the gate

A reconstruction of the Gatehouse and Barbican of the Castle at Arques in France. The barbican is an elaborate outwork covering the main gatehouse, with two drawbridges

so that their unshielded right sides were exposed to the arrows of the defenders. The end of the barbican passage was usually covered by some sort of outwork, often quite elaborate. At Goodrich in Herefordshire, for instance, it takes the form of a large semi-circular covering wall, while the two barbicans covering the gates at Conway are like small outer baileys.

The gatehouse at Warwick, built in the middle of the fourteenth century by Thomas Beauchamp, Earl of Warwick (Earl Richard's grandfather), is a good example of a compact gatehouse and barbican, built as one splendidly designed unit. The gatehouse itself is built on the traditional plan of two flanking towers joined above a narrow entrance passage. The gatehouse has three upper storeys, and tall battlemented turrets rise at each corner above the battlements of the roof. In front, two battlemented walls enclose another narrow passage leading to the gate; at the far end of these barbican walls, facing the field, is another pair of towers like a smaller gatehouse. In front of this was the drawbridge over the moat. So an attacker trying to force the gate would first have to cross the moat, then burn or batter his way through the raised drawbridge covering the first gate and the portcullis behind it. Then he would have to fight his way along the narrow passage of the barbican. Then, in front of the gate proper, there was a second gap to cross, and another raised drawbridge and portcullis to force. When he got through this he would be in the narrow passage exposed to the meurtrieres and the arrow-slits in the side walls; and at the end of the passage another portcullis. But the most interesting thing about this gatehouse is the way in which the whole approach is covered by scientifically disposed battlements, one above the other. First, the roof and turrets of the barbican; then, rising behind them, the walls and roof of the gatehouse, and then the gatehouse turrets, the first pair lower than the second, each shooting platform overlooking and supporting the one in front of it. The turrets of the gatehouse are joined by flying bridges of stone, so

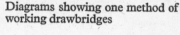

Diagrams showing one method of working drawbridges

A drawbridge in the open, as in the barbican at Arques. The bridge is fastened by chains to two great horizontal beams, each pivoted on an upright beam. The chains to the end of the bridge are fastened to the outer ends of the beams, and there is a heavy weight at the inner end of each to act as a counterpoise to the weight of the bridge. These weighted ends are drawn down by chains attached to winches. Because of the counterbalance afforded by the weights the bridge can easily be raised and lowered by two men

This shows a drawbridge in front of a gatehouse worked in the same way. The inner, weighted ends of the beams pass through holes in the wall, only the outer half projecting. When the bridge is raised, the beams set back into the slots in the wall above the gateway; similarly the drawbridge itself sets back into a recess in front of the gateway. Thus when the bridge is raised, both it and the beams are flush with the outer surface of the wall. Some drawbridges are worked more simply by means of chains passing from the outer end of the bridge, through holes in the gatehouse wall to winches inside, but this method requires more power to lift the bridge

74

that the defenders had no need to go down to roof-level and up
again in order to move from one turret to the other.

When you walk through the gate of a keep-and-bailey castle
today, one like Warwick or Dover or Kenilworth or Corfe, you
find a large, empty area of cropped grass. When these castles
were in use, what a different picture it would have been! The
whole space would have been filled with buildings, mostly of
timber but some of stone. Against the walls of the bailey you
would see lean-to shelters, some open in front and some completely closed in – stables, kennels for the hounds, byres, work-
shops of all kinds for masons, carpenters, armourers,
blacksmiths (for, make no mistake, an armourer was a highly
skilled specialist, not a blacksmith) and stores for hay and straw
like Dutch barns, dwellings for the army of castle servants and
hangers-on, open-air kitchens, a large mess-room; and in stone a
mews for the falcons, a chapel and a great hall, more airy and
luxurious than the hall in the keep to be used in the long days of
peace. Instead of grass, the ground would be of hard-packed
earth, or cobbles or even pavement – or, in some lesser castles,
probably a quagmire of mud. And instead of groups of tourists
and people picnicking in the shelter of the ruins, there would be
a great bustle and coming-and-going of working people going
about their everyday jobs. Cooking would be continual; there
would be constant feeding, watering and exercising of horses,
movement of cattle in to be milked and out to graze; armourers
and blacksmiths would be busy repairing harness for the garrison and making ironwork for the castle, shoeing horses, repairing carts and wagons – an endless hubbub of busy-ness. And
the huntsmen and verderers would be constantly busy for there
was an army of animals, hounds and hawks and horses to be

cared for, trained and exercised for hunting. Every day hunting parties would be out after deer, or small game like hares and rabbits, and on special occasions wild boar, while others would take their falcons and go after all kinds of birds. Hunting and

One of the towers of the Château of Sully-sur-Loire, showing the machicolations round its top, and along the top of the wall. Here the old roofs are still in place as they were in the fourteenth century

hawking, admittedly one of the chief pastimes of the upper ranges of feudal society, was much more of an essential part of everyday life than we might think. With so many mouths to feed, it was vital to get as much game for the pot as possible.

Though the keep-and-bailey castle was the most common all through the Middle Ages, by no means all the castles you will see in England or on the Continent will seem to be of this pattern. This is because so often during the thirteenth century castles

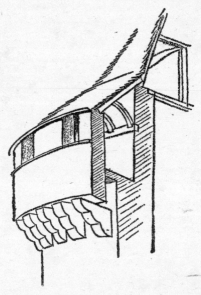

This shows how the machicolations were built

were greatly modified by additions and alterations to keep pace with new developments in siegecraft and in accordance with new ideas of defensive design. Richard Coeur-de-Lion, for instance, was an accomplished military engineer; he put many new ideas into practice, altering some existing castles such as the Tower of London, and embodying all his new thoughts in the great castle at Les Andelys in Normandy, his famous 'Château Gaillard', the castle of which he boasted that he could hold it even if its walls were made of butter. It was in fact taken only a few years later by the King of France after a not very long siege, but it fell as so many castles did because of treachery from within.

Many old castles, then, were added to during this century; new towers and gatehouse, bastions and barbicans were built, and new features appeared. The old wooden hoardings, for instance, began to be replaced by stone *machicolations*. These did in fact more or less reproduce in stone the wooden, open-decked galleries, and this machicolation is one of the typical features of the thirteenth-century castle.

But by the century's end an entirely new type of castle had developed in England, several of them being built on new sites in Wales. After Edward I had conquered the principality in 1278 and 1282, he began to build a series of great castles on a new plan to hold down his conquest, as William I had done in England 200 years before. But Edward's castles were very different from the motte-and-bailey, earthwork and stockade castles of his predecessors. Their design was, very roughly, that a central keep or citadel was done away with, and the walls and towers of the bailey were greatly strengthened. At Conway and Carnarvon, the outer walls were almost as high as those of an old-style keep, while the flanking towers had become enormous. The encircling walls still enclosed two open courts or baileys, but these were smaller than in the older, more open castles. Conway and Carnarvon were built on irregular plans to conform to the sites they stood upon, but Harlech and Beaumaris were based on the concept of a rectangular enclosure with very high, strong walls and a great drum-tower at each corner, the whole vast building enclosed within a concentric wall with bastions. There is no space here to describe these great castles in detail, but this does at least very baldly put the basic idea which was behind their design.

The same principle was in force in the design of the last real castle to be built in England – great walls linking corner towers. Late in the fourteenth century new castles of this kind were built at Bodiam in Sussex, Nunney in Somerset, Bolton and Sheriff Hutton in Yorkshire, Lumley in Durham and Queenborough in the Isle of Sheppey. The last was not quadrangular, but circular and on a completely concentric plan. This castle was totally destroyed by the Parliament in the Civil War, and no trace of it remains; all we know of it is from old drawings. The domestic buildings inside these castles were no longer either built to stand free in the bailey or built against its walls, but were all incorporated into the structure itself making for a much more logically arranged and luxurious dwelling.

After the end of the fourteenth century, the English castle declined into the fortified manor-house, where domestic care and convenience were much more important than defence. Many built during the fifteenth century kept to the rectangular plan, and most had wet moats (the old word now changed in its meaning); the only military seeming feature was the great twin-towered gatehouse. By the end of the century, castle building had ceased and the Englishman's castle had indeed become his home, for with the sixteenth century came the beginning of the great age of the English manor-house.

These remarks do not, of course, apply to Continental castles; there social conditions were different, and in Germany especially private war went on without ceasing even until the end of the sixteenth century, and castles were still very much in use. In England, on the Welsh Marches and the Scottish Border, the needs of defence and strength were still valid. On the Welsh

An aerial view of Harlech Castle. This is one of the great castles built in the time of Edward I, and shows the massive combination of the great drum towers joined in a rectangular plan by very high walls. The whole castle has in a way become a vast keep, with the gatehouse greatly enlarged and forming the most important building in the whole design. Before the main gatehouse with its huge towers is a much smaller one. There is a long bridge over the ditch, with a drawbridge (now of course a solid bridge) set at a slight angle at the inner end. There is a wall surrounding the outer edge of the ditch (the 'counterscarp') and another crowning the steep rocky sides of the inner bank. This castle is built on a high rocky hill, and the only possible approach for an assault is from the side you are looking at. You can imagine how difficult it would be to force a way across the counterscarp, then across the ditch, then up the rocky bank and the wall on top, then up and over the main wall – all the time being shot at from the walls and towers above you. All the domestic buildings at Harlech are in the block behind the main gate

Marches the old castles were needed in the fifteenth century – indeed, at this time a completely new one was built at Raglan in Monmouthshire. Very much on the pattern of Edward I's castles, it was built in the years round 1400 by Sir William ap Thomas, known as 'the Blue Knight of Gwent', and by his son Sir William Herbert, later Earl of Pembroke. It has one very striking feature which the Edwardian castles lacked – a great free-standing tower, hexagonal in plan, built upon its own mound and surrounded by a moat and a bastioned wall. It stands on its own, a castle in its own right, in front of the main castle. It was known as 'The Yellow Tower of Gwent'.

This was a late example of new building in a region where a certain amount of warfare was to be expected; but in the Border country of the North, warfare was endemic. There was no end to the cattle-lifting raids and forays of the Scots, and the counter-raids of the English. Every manor, every farm, had to be a castle. As a result, all over this country were built small castles, called *Peels*. They consisted of a simple tower, grim and solid, in a small bailey which in most cases was no more than a yard, surrounded by a high, plain, un-crenellated wall. Most of these peels were farms, and when the raiders hove in sight, the owner and his family and farm-labourers would bolt for the shelter of the peel, driving their stock into the yard. If the Scots took the trouble to stop and batter the wall down, they all took refuge in the tower, driving the cattle into the basement and themselves going into the upper floor. But the Scots rarely bothered. They were always in a hurry to get on, get as much loot as possible, and get home.

The great Age of the Castle corresponded almost exactly with the Age of Chivalry – the eleventh to the fifteenth centuries.

Warfare, even private warfare, in the fifteenth century had become quite businesslike, much more modern, with more nastiness and less glamour than it had formerly, and the development of cannon had made even the strongest castle vulnerable as it had never been before. Yet it is curious that two hundred years after the last castles had been built in England, when many were deserted and falling into ruin, they came into their own again during the Civil War of 1642–49. Several stood long sieges, pounded by cannon far more powerful than those used in the fifteenth century; and none fell by direct assault.

Chapter Four

The Castle Besieged

In war, the purpose of a castle was two-fold. It must be a place in which the leading men of a district could defend themselves against the attacks of their foes, but equally important was the fact that it was a place these same men could burst out of to attack any force which came within range of them. No commander with any sense would risk marching his force past a hostile castle; he could rarely know whether it was held in strength by a garrison large and strong enough to take the offensive, or by only two or three men-at-arms, a dozen archers and the servants. He might, assuming it to be weakly held, pass it by only to be fallen upon by a strong force; so he would always tend to play safe and either stop to besiege it or give it a very wide berth.

There were only two ways of taking possession of a castle if it was defended – by battering a way in across the barriers of its defences, or by starving it out. There was a third way – bribing someone inside to open the gate – but that does not concern us here. To sit down before a castle in regular siege took a lot of time, and required many men and a *Train* of siege *Engines*. Often it was only possible to make a quick and violent assault in the hope of breaking in, for not many medieval armies marched with siege machines in their baggage train. Where such an assault was attempted, it was a matter of rushing forward, preferably at two or three places simultaneously to distract and divide the garrison, getting somehow across the moat, hoisting long ladders against the walls, getting as many men up them as fast as possible, hacking a way off the ladders on to the wall, through the embrasures of the parapet, then getting possession of one or more towers and so gaining the bailey. Then of course there would still be the keep to take; no scaling-ladder would reach its battlement, and unless the doorway and the forebuilding could be rushed while the garrison was still trying to defend parts of the bailey, or the door itself burnt down, even an assault which carried the bailey would be unable to take the castle.

Such an assault would be beaten off by successive means of defence. First, the defenders would try to stop or at least harass the attack by means of arrows, bolts, sling-stones and probably great darts and stones hurled from the castle's own engines. When the attack got to the foot of the bailey wall, the hot oil, water, lime and so on would come into use, being poured through the openings in the hoarding or through the machicolations. When the ladders were reared against the wall, the defenders would try to push them away with long poles with forked ends. You can imagine that it would not be at all easy to push away a ladder thirty feet (nine metres) long, made of heavy timber, with fifteen or so armoured men on it, set against the wall at an angle of about sixty degrees, with a pole pushed against its very top. The weight opposed to the pole would be tremendous. Of course, if the attackers placed their ladders at too steep an angle, they would be more easily overbalanced, as they would be if their lower ends were not firmly placed. Imagine yourself in the nightmare frenzy of an assault under a defended wall; you are showered with flaming oil; arrows and stones whistle down around you, as you struggle to hold erect a great ladder. You stand on sloping, muddy ground with a ditch, probably full of water ten or so feet (three metres) deep just behind you. There are dead men under your feet, and your comrades fall round you, some silent, some screaming with pain; your armour is slimy with hot oil, agonising where it seeps into the joints or through the rings of your mail; every time you and your comrades manage to get the top of the ladder against the wall, it is pushed away. But you struggle on, and at last it settles in place at a good angle. Now your hands are free; you snatch out your weapons, sword or axe or mace, drag your shield round from your back, and with your men hurl yourself against the ladder, pressing it against the wall by your weight, holding your shield above you trying frantically to hold the ladder and your sword at the same time as you climb. Stones and arrows thump and rattle on your shield and helmet; you go up as fast as you can to get to grips with the defenders on the wall, and out of this hideous rain of missiles. Then you get level with the parapet. You are the leading man on your ladder; there seem to be dozens of warriors crowded into the embrasure before you, hacking and thrusting at you, doing everything they can to cut you down and overbalance you from your precarious stand on the ladder and send you dashing thirty feet (nine metres) or more to join the broken bodies below. There are men behind you, stout comrades you can rely on, but not one of them can do a thing to help you. Only when you force a way on to the wall and clear a space can they come up to support you. Once you are on the rampart, there is really only one way down for you – either in victory down the stair in a tower, out into the bailey; or in defeat, thrown back over into the moat.

Such an assault was a desperate business, more difficult and hazardous for the attack than for the defence, and when it was attempted as an isolated event, it was generally a failure. But when an attack on a broken-down wall came after the long preparation of a regular siege, it could be different.

There were three ways of breaking the walls of castles, each of them often being employed in succession or simultaneously. The first was to batter a breach from a distance by casting great stones against the wall from stone-throwing machines, which were called *Petrariae* or simply 'Engines'. The second method was to use battering-rams, bores or picks to make a great hole in the lower part of a wall to bring the top part down; the third was to undermine the wall: a tunnel, usually starting from some distance from the wall, with its entrance carefully camouflaged so that the defenders could not see the miners digging, was driven towards the wall; when it reached it, a large chamber – the mine proper – was dug below the foundations; as it was hollowed out, great props of timber were put in to prevent the whole thing collapsing upon the miners – just the same principle of pit-props which is used in modern coalmining. When the mine was big enough, a lot of brushwood and stuff was brought in, everything was well soaked in fat and grease and set on fire. A single man could be left to apply the fire and see that it got a hold before escaping along the tunnel, though this must have been a hazardous business because of the suffocating effect of the smoke. When the props burned through, the tower or section of wall above the mine fell in.

There were counter-measures which the garrison could take to hinder these forms of attack. Against the hurtling stones there was little that could be done in the way of direct defence; counter-attack was the only thing. Castles had their own pet-rariae from which their garrisons use to hurl stones in turn against the engines of their foes, often being able to break them up. Sometimes they shot barrels of 'Greek fire', a partly explosive and fiercely burning compound – a bit like modern Napalm – the composition of which is now forgotten. Many besieging engines were destroyed in this way. A far more glamorous method of getting rid of engines was for a small party to sally out from the castle and set fire to them personally. In this way many splendid feats of arms were performed. The ram or bore was harder to combat. The defenders could let down a great mat made of hurdles or anything else they had handy to make a sort of super shock-absorbing fend-off, but such things seldom lasted long as the ram would soon batter it through even if the attackers were unable to sever the ropes by which it was hung from the parapet. Another trick was to lower a great beam with a forked end; the fork (in theory) was dropped over the neck of the ram, thus immobilising it, but in practice this must have been almost impossible to achieve. Just imagine trying to lower a great twenty-foot (six-metre) beam, hung on ropes, swaying about as it must, over the end of another beam or tree-trunk swinging backwards and forwards thirty feet (nine metres) below you – remembering that you would have to lean out through an embrasure to do it, where you would be exposed all the time to the bolts and arrows of the attackers.

Against the mine the only defence was a counter-mine – that is, a tunnel along from your side of the wall to meet the tunnel of the attackers – depending upon your knowledge of the whereabouts of the mine. This was not difficult, when it had got dangerously near, for it was impossible to disguise the vibrations of the miners' picks under the wall. The defenders were constantly listening for their sinister sounds. There are many stories of fierce underground fights by lantern-light in the murky darkness of mine-tunnels. Sometimes, when the counter-mine had actually entered the mine-chamber, the parties of sappers, after a skirmish, would be withdrawn to allow their knightly superiors to come down and engage in most worshipful feats of arms. King Henry V went into a mine under the walls of Melun when he was besieging it in 1421, and fought with the Governor of the town, the Sire de Barbazan.

Sometimes when the besiegers had finished their mine chamber, they would call out to the commander of the garrison. When he came to the wall, or hung out of a window, he was told his castle was undermined, and asked to surrender. On some occasions he refused to believe he was undermined; then he would be invited to come down, under a flag of truce, and see for himself. This was an emminently sensible thing to do, for no besieger wanted to waste more time, effort or lives than was necessary, and since he often wanted the castle himself, or for his Lord or King, he wouldn't damage it if he could help it. When the defending commander had seen that resistance was futile, the mine was filled in again and all was well.

The engines used for these forms of attack were very simple in principle, and had changed little since the days of the ancient Assyrians in about 700 B.C. It is hard to say precisely how these were made, for the various descriptions of them in the medieval chronicles are very vague; however, we can get a general idea. First was the *Trebuchet*, for throwing the heaviest stones. There was a framework, often with small wheels to enable it to be moved, supporting two great upright posts. Working on a pivot

A Trebuchet. These were made in various sizes, some quite small, others even bigger than this. The short end carried a great weight, usually a huge basket filled with rocks; the long end, with a sling on it to contain the missile, was pulled right down by ropes working on a windlass. When this end was released, the weight at the other end came down and the sling swung up and released its missile – a large stone, generally, but sometimes a dead horse – a medieval form of germ warfare – and on a few grim occasions a prisoner or a hostage

between these posts was a long arm; the pivot was set well to one end of it, so that one end was long and the other shorter. To the end of the long arm was fastened a leather bag like the pouch of a sling, while to the short arm was attached a great weight. In preparing to shoot, the long end was pulled right down, raising the weight into the air, and fastened. Then a rock was loaded into the pouch. A peg or wedge was pulled out of the fastening of the arm, releasing it; then the weight of the short end crashed

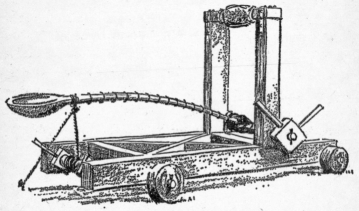

A Mangonel. This performs the same function as the Trebuchet, but is worked by a different principle. One end of the long arm is held by a web of twisted ropes, the other has a sort of spoon bowl to put the missile in. The arm is pulled down by rope and winch, and the twisted ropes are wound very tight by another winch. Then the free end is released

down, whipping the loaded long end through the arc of a circle and flinging the stone with tremendous force against its target.

An older and perhaps slightly less powerful machine was the *Mangon* or *Mangonel*. This worked by the principle of *Torsion*, that is, twisting. The same pair of upright posts held the same sort of long arm, but in the Mangonel the arm was secured right at the bottom of the posts, and the short end was much shorter. The arm was pushed through a web of twisted cords, and at its end was a large spoon-shaped bowl, or a pouch as on the trebuchet. To load it, the end was pulled right down and fastened with a rope with a release-catch. Then the web of ropes was twisted tighter and tighter by a sort of vertical capstan on the axle of the pivot. When it was as tight as it could go, the capstan was secured by wedges or a catch. Then, to shoot, the catch at the end was released; the twisted ropes sprang back, the spoon or pouch at the end of the arm was thrown violently upward, to be stopped by a cross-beam, padded in the middle, and the stone, or barrel of Greek fire or other missile was hurled forward. If you take an ordinary ruler, hold one end in your left hand, and pull back the other end with a lump of blotting paper or chewing-gum on it, and let it go, you will be using a mangonel. If you let your ruler hit something at the point where it reaches a vertical position, your lump of gum will go farther and hit its target harder.

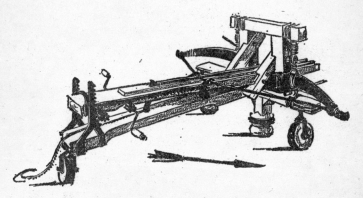

A Ballista. This is just a huge crossbow on a revolving stand, and shoots great iron bolts

Another form of artillery was a *Ballista*, a thing like an enormous crossbow on a pivoted stand. This shot great iron bolts three or four feet (about a metre) long. The Romans used them in the manner of light field guns. They had no wheels, but were mounted on vertical stands about four feet from the ground. The frame of the machine – the part corresponding to the stock of a crossbow – was pivoted on the top of the stand so that it could traverse in a complete half-circle, and it could be elevated or

A Cat, or Sow. The battering-ram is protected
by a long shed, which is covered with raw hides
to protect its timbers from fire

depressed as necessary. These could be worked by only two or three men, shooting quite fast, and could be protected by a shield fitted in front of the bow, just like the shield on an old-fashioned field-gun. These of course were anti-personnel weapons, used to pick off from long range defenders who exposed themselves on the walls, or to shoot fire-tipped bolts to burn roofs or hoardings and the houses in the bailey.

The *Ram* was just the biggest tree-trunk available, rigged up in a frame of pairs of uprights with cross-beams on top of each pair. The ram was slung on ropes from the cross-beams and between the uprights. Whenever possible, the head was made of solid iron, with a point to it. Its purpose was simply to bash and

Diagram of the ram in action at the foot of a wall

batter at the stones of the wall, but as it had to be dragged right up to the wall its use involved much preliminary work. Part of the ditch must be filled in, and the whole machine dragged forward under fire. Since men would have to work at it, swinging the ram for hours on end, they had to be protected by making a great shed to contain the whole thing. This, to strengthen it, and in an effort to make it fireproof, was covered with raw hides and sometimes with sheets of iron.

The *Pick* worked on the same principle, only instead of a great heavy trunk for battering, the tree used would be long and more slender, with a long, sharp iron spike at its end. This was used with more finesse, picking away at the cracks between the stones of the wall. The *Bore*, also working in a penthouse, was like a pick only was worked in the manner of a gigantic drill, boring away the mortar between the stones.

Another machine which was commonly used to assault the wall was a great moveable tower, which could be dragged up to the wall; there were several stages or floors in the tower, with ladders connecting them, and the front of the upper floor was a sort of large iron-faced drawbridge. Each floor would be filled with men-at-arms; when the tower was near enough to the wall, the drawbridge was lowered and a stream of men from the upper floor would rush across on to the wall, followed up by the men from the lower stages. Once such a tower actually got near enough to the wall for the drawbridge to reach across to it, the defenders had a rather poor chance; but until its fighting men had got on to the wall, the tower's position was very dangerous. It presented a large target, moving horribly slowly, to the castle's engines; their Ballistae, at such close range, could shoot the great iron bolts right through its walls of hide and wood; and though it would have been well soaked before it started, by the time it reached the wall if the day was fine the sun would have dried it, and it was susceptible to Greek fire or burning oil. The poor

A Belfry, a large moveable tower which is dragged up to the wall, full of fighting men. When it gets near enough a drawbridge is dropped over the parapet and the men inside the belfry swarm across on to the wall. The sides of the tower are covered with hides to lessen the likelihood of its being burnt

wretches who had to haul it across the uneven ground and the filled-in section of the ditch were exposed all the time, and their losses must have been heavy. To the knights and men-at-arms inside, the two or three hours' journey (for it could take as long as that) must have been a nightmare.

Another use of the tower (or *Belfry* as it was afterwards called) was to station it at some distance from the wall, and use it as a look-out post or to fill it with archers and cross-bowmen who could shoot down on to the tops of the castle walls. Henry III did this when he besieged Bedford Castle in 1224; its effect was such that the defenders never dared to take any of their armour off, so exposed were they to the shot of their opponents.

There were various nicknames given to these engines. The penthouses covering rams were often called *Cats* or *Sows* while the pick was called a *Mouse*. At the siege of Kenilworth in 1265 the belfry filled with archers (like Henry III's at Bedford forty-one years before) was called 'the Bear', and a common nickname for the Petrariae was 'Malvoisin' (Bad Neighbour). Most engines were given names, sometimes by the attackers who used them, often by the defenders who suffered from them.

It is tempting to imagine that the garrison of a thirteenth-century castle would have been very large; one thinks of bailey walls crowded with fighting men along the whole perimeter, but in fact it was not so. The peace-time garrison of most castles, even the great royal ones like Corfe or Dover or Oxford, only consisted of half-a-dozen knights, perhaps twenty other men-at-arms, fourteen crossbowmen, a chaplain, and sundry servants such as cooks, carpenters, etc. A smaller castle would have even fewer – one knight, four men-at-arms, three crossbowmen. Even in war the numbers of castle garrisons seem incredibly small.

The Pipe Roll for 1174 mentions only twenty knights at Oxford and ten knights and forty men-at-arms at Wark; and this was in a year when Henry II was battling in England against his rebellious sons. When John rebelled against his brother Richard I, when that lion-hearted monarch was a prisoner of war in Germany in 1193, the Pipe Roll gives a total garrison of only seventy-five men for both Norwich – a very large castle – and Canterbury. In 1215, when John besieged Rochester Castle, his force was opposed by only one hundred knights and men-at-arms and some crossbowmen and various servants; a year later Dover was held against the besieging force of the French Prince Louis by a much larger force. Roger of Wendover says there were 140 knights and many men-at-arms and others. But then Dover was an exceptionally important and large castle. The fact that castles could be held for such long periods against such strong besieging forces, shows how extremely efficient their defences were. In 1216, Odiham in Hampshire held out for a fortnight, defended by only three knights and ten men-at-arms. Centuries later, Corfe Castle held out for even longer against a Parliament army, complete with quite efficient cannon; and it was defended by an old lady (Lady Mary Bankes), a few old retainers and some servant-girls. The Parliamentary leader only took it because one of the servants lost his nerve and opened a gate from inside.

To end with, let us look at the accounts of some sieges. The first describes the taking of the motte-and-bailey castle of le Puiset in France, in 1111. It was besieged by the forces of King Louis the Fat, and was held by Hugh of le Puiset, its Lord. The garrison began operations by coming out and trying to drive the King's force off before he had settled down in a regular siege, but this failed and they went back behind their palisades. The next move was by the besiegers; they sent a detachment off, led by Count Theobald of Chartres, to try to storm the bailey wall round at the back. This failed too, partly because the bank was high and steep, but mainly by reason of a fierce, sudden mounted attack made by the garrison. The King's men were cut up and thrown into the ditch with considerable loss, and the horsemen rode happily back into the castle. Then after a while the main part of the besieging force, worked up to a fighting frenzy by a priest, delivered a massed attack across the ditch, they stormed up the earth bank to the palisade, and in spite of all that the defenders could do they hacked and trampled a gap in it, wrenching the great logs away, and burst into the bailey. Hugh of le Puiset and the survivors of the garrison bolted for the mound itself, the central stronghold of the castle; but they had lost many men in the fight for the bailey; they could neither defend the motte and the tower, nor escape to the open country, so they soon gave in.

Here we have a good instance of the active means a garrison could use in its defence, making fierce and sudden sorties. Even in a castle, the best form of defence was usually to attack.

The siege of Rochester Castle in 1215, when it was held by rebellious barons against King John, gives one of the rare examples of a keep being actually broken into and carried by storm. Getting past the outer defences, the besiegers were held up by the massive square tower. But the King's miners managed to drive a tunnel under one of the corners, and dug a great mine chamber. This was propped up with timber and filled with brushwood in the usual way. A royal writ addressed to the King's Justiciar, Hubert de Burgh, still survives: 'We command you that with all haste, by day and by night, you send us forty bacon pigs of the fattest and those less good for eating to bring fire under the tower. . . .' Why pigs? They were slaughtered when they reached the castle, cut up and rendered down for bacon fat. This was then smeared thickly over the timbers in the mine, and poured over the brushwood. You can imagine how that mine must have burnt. The whole corner turret came down, the King's men poured into the keep – but then they came up against the cross-wall. The defenders retreated behind this, and held out for a few more days.

When you next see Rochester keep, look at the four corner turrets. Three are the original square ones, but one is larger, and round. For many years after 1215 the keep stood shattered, one corner in ruins; but Henry III built a new tower, and there it is now. Some may say it is there because Henry III had it built, but it's really on account of those forty fat pigs.

The best example of the successful taking of a castle is the capture of Bedford Castle in 1224. It was held, in defiance of the young King Henry III, by one of John's old mercenary captains, Fawkes de Bréauté. Fawkes himself was away when the siege began, but his brother and his wife were in the castle, and held it for him against the full forces of the King. As a beginning, the garrison was solemnly excommunicated; then the siege engines were set in position. We read that a trebuchet and two mangonels were set up on the east, two mangonels on the west to shoot against the keep, and one mangonel on the north and another on the south. Two great belfrys were raised, overlooking the walls, from which crossbowmen continually kept watch on the garrison so that they had to keep their armour on and their heads down all the time. Then day after day the garrison were given no rest from the showers of bolts and the pounding of great stones against their walls. They had no intention of surrendering; they believed that if they held out, their Lord Fawkes de Bréauté would come to their help. They defended themselves fiercely, killing the Lord Richard de Argentan, six knights and over 200 men-at-arms and labourers on the engines. The King saw that there would be a long siege; he became very bitter about it, and swore that he would hang all the garrison if he took the castle.

Taken it was, in the end, in four attacks. First the barbican fell, then, losing several men, the besiegers took the bailey, and in it most of the castle's stores and provisions of corn, pigs and cattle, as well as the horses and harness, a great deal of armour and crossbows. Now they were up against the tough core of the defence – the towers and walls on the mound and the keep itself. Here the miners got to work; they brought down a length of the great wall (like a shell-keep) encircling the top of the mound. Now the attackers were inside the inner bailey, faced only by the keep, after a long and hard assault where some men were killed and ten more captured and carried off into the keep. Then the miners went to it again, and 'on the Vigil of the Assumption, towards Vespers' – that is at about four o'clock on the afternoon of 14th August – the mine was fired; the smoke poured into the inner rooms of the keep, suffocating the exhausted, starving defenders, and the tower sank upon its foundations with great cracks appearing in the walls. It was no good trying any more. The women, with Fawkes' wife who was there, and the prisoners were sent out, and the remainder of the garrison hauled up the royal banner in token of surrender. The next morning they were brought before the King; they were absolved from their excommunication, and six of the leaders were hanged with William, Fawkes' brother.

There are many records surviving which tell us of the arrangements which had to be made to organise this siege. Engines had to be carted from Lincoln, and all across Oxfordshire from Northampton; others had to be built on the spot out of timber felled in the woods of Northamptonshire and carted to Bedford. (The monks of Warden complained when the Royal foresters cut down their trees.) Carpenters were called up: the Constable of Windsor was ordered to provide horses for Master Thomas and others and their tools 'so that they shall be able to travel to us by day and by night as swiftly as they can and not tarry'. Others were sent from Lincoln and London. From London too came ropes and cables for the engines, as well as from Cambridge and Southampton; hides to make the slings and to cover the belfrys and cats came from Northampton, and from London was sent tallow to lubricate the machinery. The Sheriffs of Bedfordshire and Northamptonshire were told 'to send to us, without delay, at Bedford all the quarrymen and stonecutters in your jurisdiction, with levers, sledges, and petrariae'. Roger de Clifford, constable of St Briavels, sent miners from Hereford and the Forest of Dean. Crossbowmen came from London, and bolts for them were sent in thousands – the Bailiffs of Northampton were ordered 'as you love us and our honour, that you cause to be made, both by day and by night, by all the smiths in the town that are skilled in the art, four thousand quarrels, well barbed and well flighted. . . .' and to send them to Bedford. Fifteen thousand bolts were sent up from Corfe, too.

These items give some idea of the kind of job it was to lay formal siege to a castle; and when the King himself was present, there were extras. All his colourful and emblazoned tents and pavilions were sent up from London in carts, with all his arms and personal comforts as well as luxuries such as cinnamon, ginger, pepper, saffron and almonds, and great quantities of wine of all kinds. When it was all over, everything was packed up and sent back; the engines were dismantled and the parts sent back to the Tower of London and to Northampton, and carpenters, miners, stone workers, leather workers and labourers were able to return to their ordinary jobs. Bedford Castle was *slighted*, that is, all its defences were broken down and made useless, and Fawkes de Bréauté, deserted by his friends and his wife, went into exile.

Many castles which we can see in England today are very ruinous, more so than the passage of time seems to warrant. This is often because they were deliberately slighted, wholly or partly; but like England's ruined abbeys, which if it had not been for Henry VIII's dissolution of the monasteries might still be in a condition as good as that of the great cathedrals, many castles survived in good order until, in the Great Civil War of 1642–49, they were held, like Corfe, for the King. In order that those which had been captured should not be used against the Parliament again, and to prevent many others from being so used, their bailey walls and towers, gatehouses, curtain walls and keeps were blown up. The shattered ruins of Corfe Castle in Dorset, once one of the proudest possessions of the English crown, are at the same time a monument to the heroic defence of old Lady Bankes and her servants, and to the strength of the castle. For if you look at the scattered fragments of yellowish-grey stonework which litter the great natural mound of Corfe, you can see how strong and solid the work is; had it not been blown to pieces, it would have stood almost untouched until today, like some of the other great castles which have been more fortunate.

Index

More Beaver Books

We hope you have enjoyed this Beaver Book. Here are some of the other titles:

The Twelve Labours of Hercules The adventures of the hero Hercules, beautifully retold by Robert Newman; illustrated superbly by Charles Keeping

The Last of the Vikings Henry Treece's exciting story, in the saga tradition, about the young Harald Hardrada, King of Norway; with more superb illustrations by Charles Keeping

My Favourite Animal Stories Sad, funny and exciting stories about all sorts of animals, chosen and introduced by Gerald Durrell

Through the Fire The exciting story of how two Quaker children rescue their father from Bridewell gaol during the Great Fire of London in 1666, by Hester Burton

Old Ramon Jack Schaefer's story of an old shepherd and a boy who take their flock through the dangers of the New Mexico desert with the help of their two dogs

New Beavers are published every month and if you would like the *Beaver Bulletin* – which gives all the details – please send a stamped addressed envelope to:

Beaver Bulletin
The Hamlyn Group
Astronaut House
Feltham
Middlesex TW14 9AR

353354